America's Fly Lines

THE EVOLUTION OF THE MODERN FLY LINE FROM ITS HORSEHAIR AND SILK BEGINNINGS

By Victor R. Johnson, Jr.

Foreword By
Leon Chandler

Dedication
For Victor R. Johnson, Sr.

Published by EP Press
Copyright 2003 - Victor R. Johnson, Jr.
ISBN #0-9740531-0-4   Retail Price: $21.95

Original Cover Artwork by Diana Browning

No part of this book may be reproduced in any manner without prior written permission from the author and publisher, except for brief quotations in reviews or articles. Address all inquiries to EP Press, P. O. Box 272, Vallejo, California 94590, (707) 644-4788.

Contents

Preface 5
Foreword 7
Introduction 8

Chapter One 9
Brief history of fishing lines from ancient times until 1900

Line technology and issues: 1900—WWII
    Anatomy of a fly line
    Materials used for lines
    Braiding
    Line drying and deterioration issues
    Line floatant issues
    Lines for wet flies and nymphs

Chapter Two 23
The U.S. fly line industry: 1800—WWII

Historic line makers that are "alive and well today"
    Ashaway
    Gudebrod, Inc.
    U.S. Line Company
    Western Fishing Line Company
    Sunset

Historic line makers that are "gone but not forgotten"
    Hall Line Company
    Rain-Beau
    Weber
    Bevin Wilcox
    Norwich Line Company—S. A. Jones
        Line Company

Business combinations/conglomerates (compound line-making genealogy)
    B. F. Gladding & Company
    Horrocks Ibbotson
    South Bend

    Shakespeare
    Pflueger

    Cortland
    Newton
    Masterline—U.K.

    Berkley
    Marathon
    Fenwick
    Abu
    Garcia
    Horton Manufacturing Company
        (Bristol and Kingfisher brands)

Chain stores and catalog stores
    Montgomery Ward, Sears, and
        Western Auto
    Abercrombie & Fitch
    Herter's

Chapter Three 92
Fly lines post-WWII

New materials appear and are adopted into fly line construction.
    Nylon
    Plastic line coatings
    New manufacturing processes and
        materials appear

Chapter Four 102
Fly line standards
    The Problem
    The Solution

Chapter Five 111
The modern line (early 1960s through the early 1990s)
    Line core construction
    The PVC line coating process
    The extrusion line coating process

Technical problems remain
    Line memory versus shootability
    Coating adhesion to line core
    Flotation
    Sinking lines

Additional non-technical problems
    Environmental Problems
    Declining numbers of trout and salmon
        led to "catch and release" practices.
    Distribution of fly lines

Chapter Six 121
Scientific Anglers

Chapter Seven 128
The modern fly line from 1992—2002
    Fly fishing becomes truly international.
    Fly fishing for non-traditional species
    PVC under environmental attack
    New core and coating materials
    Clear lines and "super smooth" lines

Chapter Eight 132
The "New Manufacturers"
    Rio
    Airflo—U.K.
    Monic
    Northern Sport Fishing Products, Ltd.—
       Canada

Chapter Nine 140
Specialty lines
    Teeny
    Royal Wulff

The "Modern Specialty Retailers"
    Orvis
    L.L. Bean
    Cabela's
    Bass Pro Shops

Chapter Ten 153
"Take Care of Your Fly Line" by J. Leon Chandler

Chapter Eleven 155
Price Guide for antique fly lines

Contributors 161
References 162
Index 165
About the Author 166

Preface

My Dad and I have always been interested in "the story behind the story" and that led to our writing *Fiberglass Fly Rods*, which was published in 1996 by Centennial Publications.[1] A major theme of *Fiberglass Fly Rods* was to better understand and record the efforts of the people and the firms behind the development of modern fiberglass fly rods. Since it was the first book we had ever written, we had no idea of the extensive time and effort involved in writing a book. When it was published, we decided to do some extra fishing as a reward before starting on another book. That fishing break took four years.

FIBERGLASS FLY RODS

We have always been interested in fly lines for a variety of reasons. First and foremost is that the fly line and leader are what is between the fish and the rod and reel, which makes them all-important. Secondly, the fishing public generally tends to under-appreciate fly lines. Someone is always talking about his or her new rod, reel or latest trout fly, but seldom does anyone talk about his or her fly line. Scientific Anglers proudly notes Dave Whitlock's opinion on the importance of fly lines in a plaque in its trade show booth which states: "In my opinion, fly line is the most important component of fly fishing—it is the sport."[2] Harmon Henkin also noted this anomaly in his 1976 book, *Fly Tackle*. He stated, "As I have said before, lines are more crucial to modern fly fishing than rods, reels and whatevers. They are the central ingredient in the evolution of tackle."[3]

My Dad had personally experienced the dramatic changes in how lines were manufactured from his youth in the 1920s. I had also seen many changes in fly line technologies from my youth in the 1950s. Additionally, my Dad was a chemist and worked with synthetic coatings in the refrigeration manufacturing industry. As such, he was fascinated by the advances he saw in modern fly lines.

Many of the advances in line technology we now enjoy occurred in the late 1940s and 1950s. The key people involved with these advances are getting older, and we felt it was important to interview them firsthand. Consequently, we thought that a book on American fly lines would be an interesting and important subject. Therefore, we started writing the history of America's fly lines.

Soon after we got started, my Dad passed away. He was 84. This was a major blow to our family. Aside from losing my Dad, I also lost my favorite fishing buddy and mentor. Our family rejoices that he lived a full life of personal and professional accomplishments and caring for his family and community. This book was something we started together and I am sure he would want to see it completed. Thus, I dedicate this book to him.

I have tried to be as accurate as I could in my research for this book. In numerous cases, there was only one source still alive who is knowledgeable about a certain subject. Thus, there was no way to get several independent views on the subject and then reconcile them. If new information becomes available that revises or expands our knowledge about any subject, I will gladly include it in a future reprint.

It should also be noted that I have used the terms fisherman and fishermen in the book to describe both men and women who enjoy fly fishing.

Victor R. Johnson, Jr.

AT OCEAN WITH WIFE, DOROTHY

VICTOR R. JOHNSON, SR.

STRIPED BASS FISHING IN ARKANSAS

GRAYLING—SALMON FISHING IN ALASKA

Foreword

BY J. LEON CHANDLER

People who know me will not be surprised when I state that I think the fly line is just about the most important component in the fly angler's arsenal. My reasoning is that the fly line plays a crucial role in what I consider to be the key to successful fly fishing, namely presentation. Another key element in proper presentation is, of course, casting skill. Casting skill comes with practice, perseverance and experience. I believe that the fly line should be selected with as much or more care than any other part of the gear. One should be aware that tapered fly lines come in a variety of taper configurations — and it is important to match the taper configuration for the type of fishing that is to be done. A fly line designed for delicate dry fly trout fishing is dramatically different than one designed for casting bulky flies for bass or for saltwater species. Choose a new fly line carefully.

I have had the good fortune to have spent my entire business career on the leading edge of the fly line manufacturing business — 50 ½ years with the Cortland Line Company, Cortland, NY before retiring in 1992. So I have had a unique view of the evolution of the modern fly line — going back to the old oil-impregnated silk lines that were staples through the 1940s. As I look back through the years, I have seen many good things happen during the evolution of the modern fly line — but three events stand out, in my judgment.

1) The introduction of the first commercially successful fly line with a *synthetic* coating gave us a fly line that would not absorb water and would not become waterlogged as did the older oil-impregnated lines. That was the Cortland 333 Non-Sinkable Fly Line, introduced to the market in 1953.

2) During the late 1950s, a grand old gentleman named Leon P. Martuch developed the technique of *tapering the finish* — as compared to tapering the center braid, and the use of tiny hollow glass beads to provide buoyancy for the floating lines. Mr. Martuch then introduced these lines under the Air Cel brand for his company, Scientific Anglers in Midland, Michigan.

3) Creation of the AFTMA Standards that changed the nomenclature of identifying fly lines by *grain weight* rather than the old archaic method based on *diameter* that was previously used for the oil-impregnated silk lines. A committee from the Line Division of the American Fishing Tackle Manufacturers Association — all competitors — worked on the project for most of two years, completing the assignment in 1962.

None of us will ever know the hours, days, weeks, and years that Victor Johnson, Jr. spent doing research for this book. We, and future generations of fly anglers, all owe him a debt of gratitude. This is a book that needed to be written.

Introduction

The making of fishing lines was an early essential activity in our country's history. It is still an essential industry. Some of the firms making fishing lines in America today date back almost 200 years. For example, Ashaway was formed in 1824.

As our country has grown, fly fishing has grown from a sport for the wealthy few to a sport for millions of people. In 2001, 13 million Americans over the age of 16, went fly fishing at least once.[4] American fly fishing sales were 678 million dollars in 2000, which made it a major industry.

In 200 years there is always a lot of change in any industry. Even with America's largest firms, change is always underway. The Dow Jones listing of the 30 largest firms in America shows 49 deletions and corresponding additions to the list since its inception in 1928.[5] The fly line manufacturing industry was not immune from change over all these years. As new firms began to make fly lines, other established line-making firms were failing—somewhat like the life cycle of an aquatic insect.

The history of this ongoing change associated with fly lines in America is fascinating.

Chapter One
BRIEF HISTORY OF FISHING LINES FROM ANCIENT TIMES UNTIL 1900

One of the comforting aspects of fly fishing is its consistency. It started with a rod, a line and a fly and then later included a reel. The technology of each of these components has been improved many times over the centuries, but the general fishing approach has always been the same. This book is focused on American fly lines, but a brief discussion of historic fishing lines seems appropriate at the start of the book.

Ernest Schwiebert noted in his book, *Trout*, that the Chinese were using silk lines on thornwood rods four thousand years ago during the Chinese Bronze Age.[6] Tomb murals from the Beni Hasan architectural site in Egypt (2040-1782 BC) also show people fishing with rods and lines.[7]

FISHERMEN IN EGYPT IN CIRCA 2000 BC

Even Cleopatra, who was born in 69 BC, liked to fish.[8] Plutarch talked about Cleopatra's pleasure with fishing in his *Life of Antonius* as follows:

CLEOPATRA
Courtesy of Mary Lefkowitz

"She hath used to take delight, with her fair hand
To angle happily in the Nile, where its glad fishes
As though they saw 'twas sought to deceive them
Contended eagerly to be taken."

Fly fishing was recorded in about 200 AD by the Roman Claudius Aelian when he described the Macedonians fishing on the River Astraeus.[9] *They fasten red wool around a hook and fix to the wool two feathers that grow under a cock's wattles and which in color are like wax. The rod they use is six feet long and the line of the same length. Then the angler lets fall his lure. The fish, attracted by its color and excited, draws close and...... forthwith opens its mouth, but is caught by the hook, and bitter indeed is the feast it enjoys, inasmuch as it is captured.*

Larry Koller described information Plutarch gave in the early second century AD about fishing lines as follows: "The line should be braided horsehair, he says, and that used next to the hook should be taken from a white horse. He believed a stallion's tail hairs were the strongest and the best, the gelding's next, and the mare's least good because of the weakening effect of her urine on them." [10]

Horsehair was commonly used by most cultures for lines, although silk was used in China. Izaak Walton in his 1676 book, *The Compleat Angler*, devoted a whole chapter on directions on how to make and color horsehair lines.[11]

FISHERMEN IN WALTON'S BOOK
Courtesy of The National Sporting Library

IZAAK WALTON
Courtesy of The National Sporting Library

Walton states, *First, note, That you are to take care, that your hair to be round and free from galls or scabs, or frets; for a well-chosen, even, clear, round hair, of a kind of glass-colour, will prove as strong as three uneven scabby hairs, that are ill chosen, and full of galls or unevenness. You shall seldom find a black hair but it is round, but many white are flat and uneven; therefore, if you get a lock of right, round, clear, glass-colour hair make much of it.*

And for making your Line, observe this rule, First, let your hair be clean washt ere you go about to twist it: and then chuse not only the clearest hair for it, but hairs that be of an equal bigness, for such do usually stretch all together, and not break singly one by one, but all together.

When you have twisted your links lay them in water for a quarter of an hour, at least, and then twist them over again before you tie them into a Line; for those that do not so shall usually find their Lines to have a hair or two shrink, and be shorter than the rest of the first fishing with it, which is so much of the strength of the Line lost for want of first watering it, and then re-twisting it; and this is most visible in a seven hair line, one which hath always a black hair in the middle.

Fly fishing moved to North America with the Europeans who migrated here. Some of these wealthy early Americans were avid fly fishermen. Sir William Johnson acquired land in Sacandaga, New York, in 1769, for building a fishing lodge. Sir William had been trained in his native country, Ireland, to use a one-handed rod with a tapered horsehair line when fishing for trout.[12]

Gradually silk lines began to be the line of choice over horsehair and other materials, such as cotton and linen. In 1880, Eaton and Deller produced the first solid braided silk line with an oil dressing in England. Tapered lines also began to appear. Frederick Halford discussed the importance of pure silk tapered lines in his 1889 book, *Dry Fly Fishing*.[13] In 1908, P. D. Malloch of Perth, Scotland produced the famous Kingfisher line that set the standard of the time for oil dressed silk lines.[14] Of interest is that the Malloch name is still alive and associated with fly fishing in Perth today. There is an excellent web site with the history of P. D. Malloch at www.pdmalloch.com.

P. D. MALLOCH
Courtesy of Helen Shepherd

KINGFISHER LINE

LINE TECHNOLOGY AND ISSUES: 1900—WWII
ANATOMY OF A FLY LINE

Once tapered fly lines began to appear in the late 1800s, the terminology associated with line construction expanded so people could describe the differences between various fly lines. In their earliest form, there were three types of fly lines: Level, Double Taper and Weight Forward.

Level lines are simply level in profile from one end to the other.

PROFILE OF A LEVEL (L) FLY LINE
Line photos in this chapter are courtesy of Cortland Line Company

Double Taper (DT) lines have a thicker middle section of the line called the "belly or body" and a front tapered section called the "front taper" and an identical tapered line section at the other end of the line called the "back or rear taper." There is a short thin section of roughly 12 inches at the front end of the line called the "Tip" which allows attachment of the leader.

/Tip/ Front Taper/   Body   /Back Taper/

PROFILE OF A DOUBLE TAPER FLY LINE

Weight forward (WF) lines have the mass of fly line at the leading end of the line with a shortened "body" and "back taper."

PROFILE OF A WEIGHT FORWARD FLY LINE

Some people use other names to describe WF lines including Torpedo Taper, 3 Diameter Taper and Rocket Tapers.

There is a countless number of specialty tapers that can be designed by lengthening or shortening the three components of a fly line and also by increasing or decreasing each component's weight. Specialty tapers are very helpful in certain conditions (e.g., casting large flies, casting on windy days, delicately casting small flies, and so forth). These specialty tapers are given a name that describes their specialty use.

PROFILE OF A BASS TAPER FLY LINE
It has a short front taper to help cast heavy "bass bugs." It was one of the first specialty tapered lines developed.

After WWII, another specialty fly line was developed called the Shooting Head or Shooting Taper line. This line was designed for the long distance casting that was necessary for the large rivers in the West. Instead of being the normal length of about 90-100 feet, a Shooting Head was only about 30 feet long. A monofilament running line was attached to the back of the Shooting Head to allow it to run easily through the guides and produce long casts.

PROFILE OF A SHOOTING HEAD OR SHOOTING TAPER FLY LINE.
This line has a loop at the rear of the line to allow attachment of the running line.

Until the early 1960s, fly lines were classified by a letter system, which corresponded to their diameter. Level lines used a single letter to describe them, whereas tapered lines used letters for each of their component tapered sections.[15]

Line Diameter (inches)	Line Classification
.02	I
.025	H
.03	G
.035	F
.04	E
.045	D
.05	C
.055	B
.06	A
.065	2A
.07	3A
.075	4A

Ashaway 1948 *Sportsman Magazine*

Note: Except for quoted references, technical writing nomenclature for line diameters is used in the text of this book (e.g., 0.025 inches instead of .025 inches).

Common double taper lines for trout fishing were HDH and HCH. For a HCH line, this meant that the front taper was 0.025 inches in diameter at its end, the body or belly section was twice as thick at 0.05 inches in diameter and the back taper was again 0.025 inches in diameter at its end.[16]

In contrast, a common weight forward dry fly line (also called torpedo taper or 3 diameter taper) was a HCG line. It had about 9 feet of front taper that was 0.025 inch diameter at its end, about a 15 foot belly or body section of 0.05 inch diameter, and a back taper of about 4 feet that was 0.03 inch diameter at the end.[17]

MATERIALS USED FOR LINES

At the start of the Twentieth Century in the U.S., cotton, linen and silk were the basic materials used for making lines. Cotton came from the U.S., linen came from Ireland and silk came from Japan. As technology advanced, so did material science for fly lines with the introduction of nylon (invented in 1934), Dacron, Kevlar and other new materials. A brief discussion of the materials used to make lines between 1900 and WWII follows:

Silk

Silk originated in China in c. 2700 BC.[18] Chinese tradition says that Hsi ling shi, the bride of the Emperor Huang Ti, learned how to rear caterpillars on mulberry leaves and then unwind their silk from their cocoons. The Chinese tried to protect their silk making process, but over time the process reached Japan, India and ultimately the West in the Eleventh and Twelfth Centuries. In 1565, there were approximately 10,000 silk looms in Genoa, Italy alone.[19]

Silk is a fiber extruded by certain kinds of moths and spiders. A silkworm is a common name for the silk producing larvae of several species of moths—the most notable being *Bombyx mori*. In spite of their common name being silkworms, the larvae that make silk are not worms. They are caterpillars. The caterpillar larvae feed on Mulberry leaves and other similar materials as they mature. Each larvae has two internal glands that secrete a clear fluid which then joins together into a single thread and becomes hard when it reaches the air. This is silk. Silk is used by the larvae to make their cocoons during their final pupating stage before becoming moths.

The fine silk thread that is part of a cocoon is very long—up to a mile in length. This contrasts with cotton fibers, which are only an inch or two in length. Just before the pupae become moths, most of them are killed and the silk around the cocoons is removed by a machine reeling process. In this reeling process, the filament ends of typically 4-20 cocoons are pulled together. Then, the combined filaments are wound together on a reel. In the process

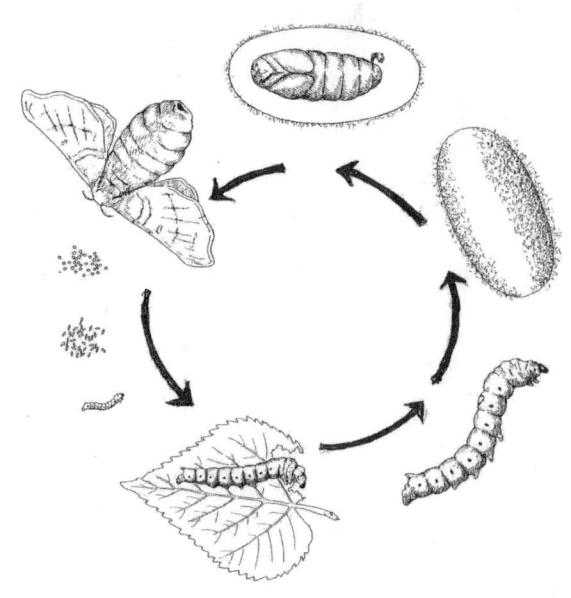

A SILKWORM'S LIFE CYCLE
Courtesy of Macclesfield Museums Trust

CHINESE WOMAN REELING SILK
(CIRCA 1850)
Courtesy of Macclesfield Museums Trust

of reeling, the individual filaments adhere to each other because of the natural gum on their surface. The reeled material (called raw silk) appears to be a single thread, but is actually composed of individual filaments from each cocoon being reeled together. The raw silk is subsequently twisted into strands sufficiently strong for weaving or knitting.

A selected number of pupae are allowed to become moths to ensure continuation of the species and the silk-making process.

Silk Gut

The silkworm was also the key in the making of silk "gut." Gut was a popular leader material as well as an important surgical suture material. In the process of making gut, the pupae were killed just before their cocoon state. The bodies of the silkworms were then opened and the thread material that was intended to make the cocoon was removed from their silk glands. The thread material was then stretched to create a silk "gut" filament. In early days before chemical processing and sizing dyes were invented, the gut and associated attached body components were drawn through the teeth of the peasants who processed it in order to make filaments.[20]

Silk gut used for leaders came from a variety of places. Spanish gut generally was considered the best leader material. In contrast to today's leaders, gut leader material required routine maintenance. Before usage, it needed to be presoaked (preferably in a glycerin solution) and then also dried after usage as it was prone to rotting.

Arguably, the first mention of silkworm gut being used for fishing was in John Saunders' 1724 London book on fishing.[21] Gut was actively used for leader material for over 200 years. Edward R. Hewitt's *Handbook of Fly Fishing* from 1933 described the need to search for and buy round gut as contrasted to flat gut.[22]

SILKWORM GUT TAPERED LEADER

Round gut was significantly stronger than flat gut. Hewitt generated a table for the average strengths of gut as follows:

Diameter of Gut	Breaking Strength in Pounds-Wet
0.005 inches	1-1.50 pounds
0.006 inches	2-2.25 pounds
0.008 inches	2.50-3 pounds
0.010 inches	3-3.50 pounds
0.012 inches	4-4.50 pounds
0.014 inches	4.50-5 pounds
0.016 inches	6-6.50 pounds
0.018 inches	7-7.50 pounds
0.020 inches	8-8.50 pounds

Nylon was invented in 1934, but the early nylon leaders were very limp and simply did not perform very well. Fly fishermen continued to use silk gut until the nylon leader manufacturers improved nylon to a point where it was as good as silk gut (i.e., c. 1960s).

Other types of "gut or intestine" materials also have a long history of use for medical sutures, strings for musical instruments and to a minor degree for fishing leaders. Cats (before their use was outlawed in many countries) and sheep have commonly been the source of the gut material for these uses.

IZAAK WALTON SILKWORM GUT LEADERS

Cotton

Cotton has been an important fiber for a long time dating back thousands of years before the Christian era (BC). Evidence exists that dates cotton to 6000 BC in Peru and Mexico and 3000 BC in East Africa and Southern Asia.[23] Until the Arabs brought cotton to Spain in the Middle Ages, wool was the only European fiber for clothing.[24] Cotton was slow to come to England because the wool manufacturers passed a law in 1720 making the manufacture or sale of cotton cloth illegal. This law was repealed in 1736.

Cotton fiber comes from the cotton boll, which is a seed pod left after the cotton flower dies. Each boll can contain about 30 seeds and up to 500,000 fibers of cotton. Harvested cotton is "ginned," the process in which the fibers are separated from the rest of the boll material. Then, the cotton fibers are spun into yarn and threads. Ginning and spinning were done in ancient times by hand. In 1765, James Hargreaves of England invented a mechanical spinning jenny. This invention was followed in 1793 when America's Eli Whitney invented and patented a mechanical cotton gin. These two inventions revolutionized cotton manufacturing.

ILLUSTRATION FROM WHITNEY'S PATENT

Although silk fly lines became more popular over time, cotton tapered fly lines were still being used until the 1930s due to their relative inexpensive cost compared to silk.[25]

Linen

Linen is one of the earliest fiber products known to civilization.[26] Linen can be dated back 6000 years or more as many of the mummies of ancient Egypt had linen wrappings. Linen comes from the flax plant, which can be grown in many parts of the world.

The flax plant creates some of the strongest vegetable fibers in nature.[27] The fiber used for linen comes from the skin of the flax plant that surrounds the core of the plant's stem. Every part of the flax plant is used today, making it arguably the most environmentally friendly fiber in the world.

The Phoenicians brought flax to Europe before the birth of Christ. Fine linen has traditionally been associated with Ireland, Bel

FLAX PLANT
Courtesy of The Linen House

gium, France and The Netherlands. Linen fishing lines have a long history of use—especially in saltwater sport fishing.

BRAIDING

Lines are normally made by twisting or braiding. In their simplest form, lines are made by twisting a number of strands together. Rope and twine (e.g., kite string and masonry lines) are common examples of twisted products. Generally, twisted products have a low number of strands (often 3) that are twisted together, although some of the early cuttyhunk linen lines were twisted products and had substantially more strands. In early America, rope and line were twisted by hand. Today, twisting machines perform the same function.[28]

Braiding is a different process from twisting. We all have seen girls and women braid their hair. Braiding of fishing lines from cotton, linen, silk or one of the new synthetic fibers is basically done the same way. Braided products generally have more strands than twisted products (often 16 for a fly line). A formal definition of braids is that they are textile compositions made with yarn thread crossing in diagonal direction.[29] Each thread intertwines the diagonal threads it crosses one from above and one from below. Braids come in two general kinds—round and flat. Round braids have a round cross section (e.g., lines, cables, and so forth) while flat braids are laces, such as shoe laces.

Braiding a large number of threads together by hand is difficult to do. Thomas Wattford developed the first braiding machine in 1748 and within a few years there were numerous firms using braiding machines in Western Europe.[30] Braiding machines soon came to the U.S. In the U.S., firms like New England Butt Company historically made braiding machines. Braiding machines are exceptionally hardy and many braiding machines over 100 years old are still used today to braid fishing line.

BRAIDING MACHINES
Courtesy of U.S. Line Company

Even using braiding machines, the making of tapered fly lines was always a slow and labor intensive process. Whereas, level braided lines could be made by machine in long continuous lengths, tapered lines were different. To get a tapered line, the braiding machine operator had to periodically stop the braiding machine and either cut or insert a line to decrease or increase the line size. No two lines were ever exactly the same due to this laborious process. Consequently, the output of tapered lines from this process was incredibly small. A single braiding machine was only able to make about five and one half feet per hour of tapered fly line.[31]

After the silk lines were braided it was common to apply some form of finish to "waterproof" them because silk absorbs water. Some manufacturers used an enamel coating on their lines. These enameled coatings were prone to cracking, which then allowed water to absorb into the silk portion of the line.

ENAMELED FLY LINE

Gradually, the line manufacturers found that the best finish came from the use of waterproofing oils. Linseed Oil was commonly the oil that was used. On premium grade lines, as many as 12 different coats of oil were required. After each coating, the line was passed through a heated tower and then the line was allowed to dry for 5-15 days. Machine brushing and sanding was often utilized to remove excess waterproofing material. Lines were also often baked in ovens to harden their finish. From start to finish, it might take an elapsed time of up to three months to make a waterproofed fly line using this process.[32]

LINE DRYING AND DETERIORATION ISSUES

Today, when we are through fishing, we simply take our fly reel and let it dry, if it has gotten wet. We then just store it for the next outing. We generally pay little or no extra attention to the line on the reel. In the past, this was not the case. Lee Wulff described line care in 1948 as follows:

Some lines are safely stored upon the reels but others should be hung loosely on wood pegs or wound around a line dryer that will hold them in position for good ventilation in such a way that they will not develop kinks or twists. Lines are likely to rot if they are confined in a damp place without a free flow of air or put away still wet from the last fishing trip of the season.[33]

Linen line was commonly used for saltwater fishing. It was subject to another deterioration factor—sunlight.[34] Consequently, drying of linen lines in strong sunlight was discouraged with drying most desirably being carried out in a cool dark place permitting a free circulation of air. It was also important to dry the entire wet portion of the line. Linen lines generally had an equal amount of wet line on the reel from wicking (water being absorbed up the line) as there was wet line from being in the water.

TYPICAL LINE DRYER

LINE FLOATANT ISSUES

Although line manufacturers made their fly lines for dry fly fishing as waterproof as possible, silk and cotton lines still needed to be dressed (greased) with a floatant at the start of each fishing day. Arguments between fishermen over what was the best dressing could go on for hours. In England, deer fat was the early favorite for dressing and had a strong following up to WWII.[35] Over time, some groups of fishermen liked deer fat, while others preferred: bear fat, mineral oils, paraffin compounds, turpentine blends, and so forth.

The selection of the correct line dressing was compounded by all the marketing claims of "being the best" associated with most commercial line dressings. Many line companies had their own brand of dressing and some famous fly fishermen like Edward Hewitt made and sold their own special blends (e.g., Hewitt's blend cost 30 cents a box in 1933.)[36] "Red Tin" Mucilin from England was manufactured by Thos. Aspinall Ltd., Carlton Chemical Works, Bolton. It was a commonly used line dressing both in England and America. Note: Mucilin is harmful to modern synthetic lines.

MUCILIN LINE DRESSING

P & K LINE DRESSER AD FROM 1947

Selecting the right dressing was just the start of the process. The problem was that over the course of a day of fishing with oiled silk lines, even when properly dressed, they began to sink just like a dry fly sinks over time. Simply applying more dressing to a wet line increased the chance of trapping moisture inside the line and causing fungal rot.

When his line began to sink, a fisherman had several options: 1) He could switch to another reel and a new line—if he was fortunate enough to have one. 2) He could remove the line from the spool and wait for it to dry. 3) He could reverse the line on the reel and use the portion of the line that was not waterlogged. 4) He could quit fishing for the day. Again, the harsh reality was that the wet line needed to be dried correctly and redressed before fishing the next day.

Consequently, it was highly recommended that after a line was dried, that it be cleaned outdoors with a naphtha-soaked cloth to remove dirt and accumulated line dressing. Then, the line was drawn through the dressing applicator and dropped in large loops on clean newspaper. A second method was to lay the line out to its full length and apply dressing in a continuous operation from end to end. Dressing was to be applied liberally, then it was to be "worked into the line" with one's fingers and finally any excess dressing was to be removed.[37]

HOW TO CLEAN AND DRESS A FLY LINE...

Use naptha, carbon tetrachloride or kerosene to dampen (NOT SOAK) a soft cloth. Wipe the line with one cloth and dry it at once with another as you go. Don't get the line too wet or you will destroy its finish. Work outdoors with the line stretched between trees, preferably.

Rub commercial dressing on a SILK LINE with fingers only (NO PAD). Wipe surplus off with a soft cloth. Rub parafin wax on NYLON LINE then rub it down with paper. NEVER dress a dirty line.

HOW TO REPAIR A TACKY FLY LINE....

Oil finished silk fly lines sometimes become sticky or tacky after being used for a while. You may extend their usefulness for a few cents.

Soak tacky lines in a creamy solution of whiting and water for several days. After drying for a day, rub it with a soft cloth then polish with a chamois. Apply dressing.

HOW TO CLEAN AND DRESS A FLY LINE (1953)
Courtesy of Barnes & Noble

HOW TO REPAIR A TACKY FLY LINE (1953)
Courtesy of Barnes & Noble

The drying and dressing challenges were not the only issues with oil-finished silk fly lines. They also tended to become sticky or tacky and there was also a process for repairing them.

Finally, the oil impregnation in the line could be damaged. Thus, there was also a process for refinishing a fly line.

HOW TO REFINISH A FLY LINE (1953)
Courtesy of Barnes & Noble

Today's fly fisherman is truly fortunate to have lines that always float and, for all intents and purposes, require no maintenance.

LINES FOR WET FLIES AND NYMPHS

Dry fly fishing was the standard method of fly fishing until approximately 1900. An occasional fish would be caught on waterlogged flies and lines that were below the surface, but "proper" fly fishing etiquette had always mandated the use of dry flies. Relatively little was known about the aquatic biology that takes place in a river or lake. Today, we know that subsurface nymphs are estimated to be more than 90% of a trout's normal diet.[38]

In the late 1800s, G.E.M. Skues broke tradition and started using subsurface flies in England. He is generally considered the father of nymph fishing in both England and the U.S.[39] Starting in the 1920s, Edward Hewitt, the ardent American angler, began to design and use nymph flies. James Leisenring wrote his famous *The Art of Tying the Wet Fly* in 1941.

Over time, wet fly and nymph fly fishing became accepted as another "proper" form of fly fishing—although heated discussions among fishermen are still common regarding the topic.

As subsurface fly presentations became more popular, line designers and manufacturers began to supply more and more specialized lines for nymphing and wet fly fishing.

Chapter Two

THE U.S. FLY LINE INDUSTRY: 1800—WWII

Historically, commercial fishermen made their lines during their off season. With the advent of machines to process natural fibers such as silk, cotton and linen into line components, a commercial line industry began to emerge. At the beginning, rope and lines were often made on a "line walk" in which strands were laid along a path and then twisted together with the aid of a large wooden wheel. Long lines required long "walks." Ashaway's "line walk" in circa 1854 was about 480 feet long (i.e., over 1 1/2 football fields in length).[40]

On a historical basis, fishing solely for sport was a luxury few could afford. As people's basic needs were more easily met due to the success of the industrial revolution, angling for pleasure evolved. Philadelphia's Schuylkill Fishing Club was formed in 1732.[41] These new sport fishermen gravitated toward lines made by professional line manufacturers. Many of the firm's names we recognize for sport fishing lines were formed in the early 1800s (e.g., Gladding in 1816 and Ashaway in 1824).

By the end of the 1800s, America consisted of thirty-eight states, and a population of nearly sixty million people. Approximately 65 percent of the population lived in rural areas.[42] With so many people living in rural areas, fishing was a major part of the fabric of America's society.

The early line manufacturers in America were the source of fly lines for most sport fishermen and their history is fascinating.

Historic line makers that are "alive and well today" through continual adjustment of their products in response to the market's needs. They were major fly line manufacturers at one time, but they are not today. Note: (date) is the date the firm was started

Ashaway (1824)
Gudebrod, Inc. (1870)
U.S. Line Company (mid-1800s)
Western Fishing Line Company (c. 1930)
Sunset (1932)

ASHAWAY

Captain Lester Crandall was a fisherman in Rhode Island (RI). He was a descendent of an early American family of Crandalls that had lived in America since the mid-1600s. Captain Crandall, like the fishermen of his era, made lines during the off season through the traditional "line walk" method. In 1824, he decided he could make a better living as a line maker than as a fisherman and founded what is now known as Ashaway Line and Twine Manufacturing Company (Ashaway). The name "Ashaway" referred to the nearby Ashaway River, which is located in the southwest corner of RI. The current Ashaway facilities in Ashaway, RI are still very near the original site of Captain Crandall's first line-making operations.[43]

Captain Crandall brought a son into Ashaway in 1854 (H. L. Crandall) and the Crandall family has run the firm ever since. Currently, Kathryn Crandall is Ashaway's president and represents the sixth generation of Crandalls to lead the firm.

EARLY VIEW OF ASHAWAY PROPERTY
Courtesy of Ashaway

A. JULIAN CRANDALL
Courtesy of Ashaway

Ashaway's line terminology is often tied closely to early American terminology. Virtually everyone in America has been taught that the Pilgrim Fathers started the first settlement of Europeans in New England in 1620 at Plymouth Rock in Plymouth, Massachusetts. This is not 100% accurate. Arguably, the first settlement of Europeans in New England was actually made in 1602 by Captain Gasnold when he landed on an island that became known as "Cuttyhunk." This island was a sportsman's paradise that attracted many sportsmen over the ensuing two centuries. One wealthy group of sportsmen started the Cuttyhunk Fishing Club in 1865. They liked the twisted hand-laid linen lines made by Ashaway and asked that Ashaway name their lines after their Club. The association of the Cuttyhunk Fishing Club with Ashaway's "Original Cuttyhunk Lines" is now generally forgotten. The word "cuttyhunk" became a generic term associated with fine linen fishing lines.[44]

In 1903, another Crandall (A. J.) took over the reigns at Ashaway and made a watershed decision that the future of the firm was going to be oriented toward the sportsman—rather than the commercial fisherman. Commercial fishing lines were totally discontinued by 1939. Ashaway even let some famous individuals and sportsmen name some of their line series. Zane Grey, the popular novelist and avid deep-sea fisherman, had a series of linen lines named after him. The rugged Zane Grey linen line had 54 threads in it.

When WWI started, Ashaway switched to war production, making, among other things, silk cords for powder bags.

ASHAWAY CRANDALL'S AMERICAN FINISH LINE

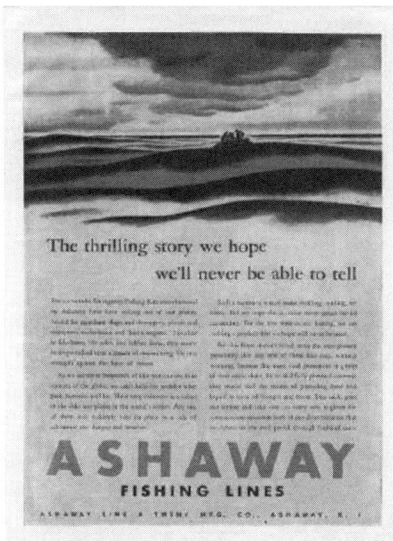

ASHAWAY 1944 WWII AD

Although Ashaway's first silk fly lines were produced in 1906, it was not until after WWI that most Americans began to switch from British tapered silk lines such as the popular Kingfisher and King-Eider lines to American made lines. In 1924, Ashaway introduced the Crandall's American Finish Line. Arguably, it was the first generally accepted silk fly line made in America that was equal to or better than the British lines at the time. It had a distinctive soft finish that was very popular. This was followed in 1926 by the introduction of tapered silk fly lines.

It is interesting to note that prior to WWII, Ashaway used a Native American good luck symbol on the boxes of some of their lines. Later, Adolph Hitler took the same symbol and turned it into the hated swastika image.

NATIVE AMERICAN SYMBOL ON ASHAWAY LINE CONTAINER

WWII saw Ashaway again switch to war production making surgical sutures, shroud ropes for parachutes and nylon glider tow ropes. Julian T. Crandall (J. T.), a great grandson of the firm's founder, was at the firm's helm. Ashaway also helped develop the Emergency Fishing Kit for lifeboats and life rafts, which were so important to allied personnel adrift in the oceans. Gifford Pinochot, former Governor of Pennsylvania, led the Emergency Fishing Kit development team that included J. T. Crandall. This team found that nearly all saltwater fish could be safely eaten raw and that the life sustaining lymphatic fluid could be squeezed from them when fresh water was not available. More than 600,000 Emergency Fishing Kits were made before the war's end.

Nylon had been invented in 1934 at a DuPont laboratory by a research team directed by chemist, Wallace Carothers.[45] Nylon did not rot and lose its strength like natural fibers such as silk or linen. It could also be finely extruded into unlimited lengths. On January 20, 1939, Ashaway started marketing Ashaway Nylon Bait Casting Line, which was the first commercial product made of nylon. Women's nylon hose did not appear in stores until May 15, 1939.[46] Nylon became the fly line material of choice post-WWII, as nylon lines did not require the degree of care needed to promote long wear as silk lines did.

Crandall's American Finish and J. T's Soft Finish silk lines were Ashaway's flagship pre-1940 and pre-nylon lines. A number of new lines were introduced after WWII including: Nylon, Ashaway Golden Nylon, Ashaway XF-100, Ashaway XF 200, Silver Knight (circa 1957 line with an aluminized "friction free miracle metal" surface) and Ashaway Griffin (1960s era line).

ASHAWAY J. T'S SOFT FINISH LINE

ASHAWAY NYLON LINE

ASHAWAY LINE WITH DISTINCTIVE CONTAINER

The price of an Ashaway nylon line could fit into any fisherman's budget in 1948. An Ashaway Nylon series level line in a 25-yard coil cost between $1.75 (size H) and $3.25 (size B). More expensive 30-yard single taper lines cost $6.50 regardless of size. 30-yard double taper lines ranged from $8.50 (size HEH) to $10.00 (size GBG). Torpedo-Head 3 taper lines ranged from $8.50 (size HEG) to $11.00 (size GAF). All of these lines were braided from DuPont Nylon and were finished with a composition soft finish.

In 1948, Ashaway also made a solid nylon leader stock called "solid nylon" to compete with Spanish gut. 10-yard coils of 4-pound test nylon leader material cost $1.50.

Ashaway started a new firm called Ashaway, Inc. in 1946 to market a wide number of non-line products including reels, lures, and sunburn creams.[47] Sport fishermen regularly read Ashaway's sports magazine called the *Ashaway Sportsman* which featured their products and interesting fishing stories. Ashaway continued to be a leader in the fly line business through the 1940s and 1950s. In 1952, when Dacron was introduced, Ashaway was one of the first firms to make fishing lines from it.

The invention in the early 1950s of truly floating lines was a dramatic change in the fly line business. Silk and nylon fly lines had inherent physical property limitations that would not allow them to compete with the new synthetic-coated lines. Ashaway initially responded by having Scientific Anglers make the new plastic floating lines for them.[48] Gradually, Ashaway stopped making its own brand of fly lines.

Ashaway, as it had done so many times since 1824, then refocused on other markets. It now makes over 75 million yards annually of suture thread, tennis strings (Andre Agassi is a customer.). Ashaway also still makes braided nylon cores for fishing lines for outside clients. In 1999, Ashaway produced 250 million yards of line products, which was more than enough to circumvent the globe five times. Ashaway is truly an American institution of which we can all be proud. They have an excellent web site at www.ashawayusa.com.

GUDEBROD, INC.

Gudebrod started with the Gudebrod family who emigrated from Germany to the U.S. in the mid-1800s. They settled near Windsor Locks, Connecticut (CT). There were seven Gudebrod brothers whose ages spanned 30 years. The oldest brother was Christian Gudebrod and in 1885, he purchased an existing silk mill in Windsor, CT and renamed it the Champion Silk Company. Over time, two other brothers joined the business and circa 1893 they bought a second silk mill in Bethlehem, Pennsylvania (PA). In 1895, they moved their entire operations to Pottstown, PA and they renamed the company the Gudebrod Brothers Silk Company. The firm still resides in Pottstown and is known today as Gudebrod, Inc. (Gudebrod).[49] Gudebrod lists 1870 as the official date of their founding.

EDWARD GUDEBROD (YOUNGEST OF SEVEN BROTHERS) IN FRONT OF GUDEBROD PLANT
Courtesy of Gudebrod, Inc.

By WWI, Gudebrod was producing a wide range of silk products (thread, dental floss and surgical sutures). Its silk surgical suture was actively used during WWI. In WWII, in the war area called the "Southeast Theatre," the heat and humidity of that area caused silk and linen suture material to rot. Gudebrod helped develop a substitute nylon suture. It also produced a glass capsule that had a needle and some silk thread that went into field packs for emergencies.[50]

Prior to WWII, Gudebrod occasionally made braided casting lines on a private label basis for other manufacturers. This changed in 1945 when it entered the sport fishing line business under its own label. Gudebrod started making Gudeline nylon fishing line. In 1946, it was marketing its Fly Queen nylon fly lines. It also was making level and tapered silk fly lines.

Gudebrod's range of fly lines grew rapidly. For example, in 1947, it was marketing:

- GudeKing tapered and level silk lines—oil-impregnated and vacuum processed (these flagship tapered lines sold for $11.00.)
- GudeBlend silk level lines—oil-tempered
- GudeSpider silk level lines—oil-tempered
- Reel Lucky silk level lines—plasticized oil lines that were its most economical line.
- GudeQueen nylon tapered and level lines—oil-impregnated and vacuum processed. (These lines sold for $8.85.)

By 1948, you could get the GudeKing silk and GudeQueen nylon fly lines in torpedo tapers. Gudebrod's economical nylon GudeFlite fly line followed in 1949. In 1953, it produced the nylon G-5 Floater, which did not need dressing. (See photo next page.)

GUDEBROD FLY KING SILK LINE

In the late 1960s, Gudebrod stopped making oil-finished fly lines and gradually went out of the fly line manufacturing business. In the late 1970s, Gudebrod made an arrangement with Masterline of the U.K. to distribute Masterline fly lines in the U.S. This relationship ended in the 1980s.[51]

GUDEBROD MASTERLINE FLY LINE

GUDEBROD G-5 FLY LINE (1953 AD)

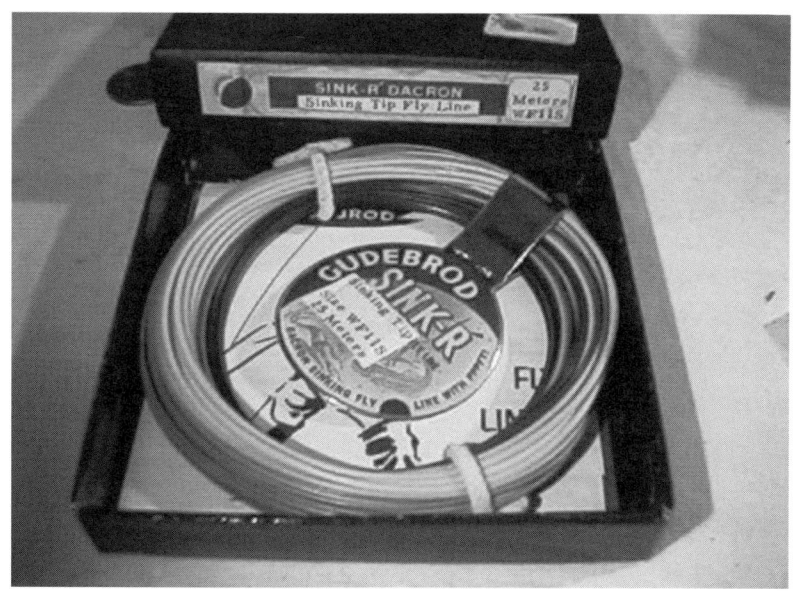

GUDEBROD SINK-R DACRON LINE

Gudebrod's exit from the manufacturing fly lines was counterbalanced with its continued penetration into silk fly tying thread business, in which it is arguably the largest manufacturer in the U.S. today. It also makes backing for fly lines today as well as rod winding thread. Additionally, Gudebrod has always had a diverse manufacturing business and continues to make dental floss, medical cords, goods for the aerospace industry and silk thread—see www.gudebrod.com. It should be noted that there are still descendents from the Gudebrod family in active management positions within the firm. This is a testament to the lasting strength and continuity of the firm.

U.S. LINE COMPANY

Westfield, Massachusetts was famous in the mid-1800s for making horse whips. In 1866, the 30 major whip manufacturers in Westfield made an estimated 95% of all the whips manufactured in America. Westfield's U.S. Whip Company was a major manufacturer and by 1892 produced the amazing number of 25,000 whips per day.[52]

U.S. WHIP 1906 STOCK CERTIFICATE
Courtesy of Scripophily.com

The advent of the automobile began to greatly diminish the need for horse whips. Firms either changed their focus or went out of business. In 1926, U.S. Whip Company chose to start making sport fishing lines and subsequently changed its name to U.S. Line Company (U.S. Line). Its 1928 fly lines came in an aluminum leader box, which could be used to hold leaders after the line was removed.

The Comstock family was a major early stockholder. In U.S. Line's early fishing line manufacturing period, its lines were made from cotton from the U.S., linen from Ireland and silk from Japan. U.S. Line also sold rods and reels made by others. By 1935, it had a full line of enameled Japanese silk fly lines including:

- True Taper—a double taper line that was its flagship tapered fly line
- Gold Metal—a level fly line made from 16 strands of braided silk, which was its flagship level line.
- Stream Line—a green colored level silk line
- Level Best—a mahogany colored level line
- Japanoid—a black and white colored level line
- Professor—a level line with more white than black strands
- Golden Spinner—an ivory colored level line
- Royal Trout—a level line with a checked pattern
- Black Beauty—a black level line

HIGHEST QUALITY ENAMELED SILK FLY LINES

LEVEL BEST

A BEAUTIFUL, SMOOTH, FLAWLESS, FLEXIBLE LINE

16 strands of flawless "Premium" Silk, expertly braided, at exactly the correct speed and tension for maximum strength, into a line the equal or superior of any level line made, imported or domestic. Smooth as glass, extra flexible and non-kinking, very easy to cast, whether with flies, bass bugs, or spinners. Ideal for strip casting with fly-and-spinner combination, fly rod lures, etc., etc. A great line for still fishing or trolling as it doesn't "kink up," or "wrap around." Rich, dark, luxurious Mahogany color. Specify whether you want 25 yard coils, 4 connected in box, or put up 33⅓ yard coils, 3 connected in box.

Sizes H G F E D
Test   14 18 24 30 38 lbs.

STEEL HEAD ASSORTMENT

A QUICK SELLING COUNTER SELECTION

Patterns, sizes, colors, all selected from our very best selling enamel lines, in order to make up an assortment for a quick turnover. Especially picked out for rapid sale by dealer who doesn't care to stock large quantity of enamel lines. 600 yards of Enameled Fly Line in a six compartment fancy box giving excellent display. Assortment contains four 25 yard coils each brand as follows:

Swiftwater G, 16 lb. test
Professor H, 14 lb. test
Japanoid G, 18 lb. test
Hardy Favorite H, 14 lb. test
Radio Special I, 12 lb. test
Green River F, 24 lb. test

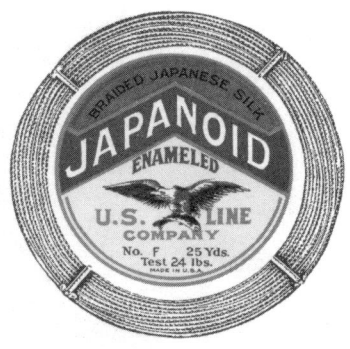

JAPANOID

A FAMOUS "BLACK AND WHITE"

A wonderful level line for fly casting — also exceptional for resisting the wear and tear of trolling, still fishing, bass bugging, and "strip" casting. The most popular of all fancy patterns, black and white check. Sixteen super-perfect Premium silk strands braided just right for strength, endurance, and flexibility. The enamel, wonderfully smooth and hard to crack, chip, or strip, is impregnated into this mighty good line by secret pressure process. A real seller. A real hit with anglers. 25 yards coils, 4 connected, 100 yards in box.

No.   I H G F E D
Test 12 14 18 24 30 38 lbs.

U.S. LINE 1935 CATALOG
Courtesy of U.S. Line Company

Enameled lines were prone to a variety of waterproofing problems due to cracking, peeling, and checking in their finish. In 1936, U.S. Line discontinued its American Enamel Finish and went to "an extra flexible New Process Finish." All of the 1936 line series remained the same with the exception of the type of finish on them.

U.S. LINE TRUE TAPER LINE

U.S. LINE GOLDEN SPINNER SILK LINE

By 1938, U.S. Line was marketing a Quick Taper series of torpedo-tapered lines which was another high-end line to go along with its flagship True Taper series. This was followed in 1942 with the Supervisor series that came both in level and tapered line configurations. The Mahogany King silk double tapered, high-end line also followed in the traditional brown color of English fly lines.

During WWII, U.S. Line made parachute cords and proudly advertised that fact in *Field & Stream* magazine in 1943.

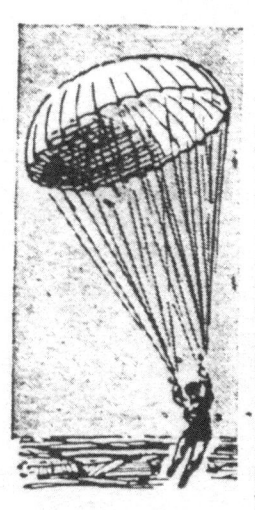

U.S. LINE 1943 AD

With the invention of nylon, the Supervisor series was made available in tapered and level nylon in 1949. By 1958, U.S. Line was selling its popular Queen of the Waters nylon series. Other popular fly line of this period included the Westfield nylon series and the Professor Dacron series.

Over time, U.S. Line discontinued making its own fly lines. It has since developed a significant market place niche in making fresh and saltwater deep trolling lines.[53] Many of these trolling lines are lead core or wire lines. U.S. Line is arguably the world's largest braider of lead core trolling lines. Additionally, it makes Dacron backing for fly lines and other casting and big game lines. U.S. Line has an excellent web site at www.usline.com, which shows the full breath of the firm.

U.S. LINE MAHOGANY KING LINE

WESTERN FISHING LINE COMPANY

Western Fishing Line Company (Western) evolved from a Los Angeles, California (CA) company making laces for corsets and shoes. David Lippy took over the company and added braided fishing lines to the business in the late 1930s. In 1939, the plant was moved to Glendale, California. Sunny California allowed Western to have its casting pool on the roof of its factory—something that would have never worked in colder climates.

The start of WWII created some special challenges for America's line-making industry. Oriental silk for parachutes and parachute cord lines to suspend the parachutist was not readily available. Consequently, many airmen flew without parachutes during the early part of the war. The U.S. Air Force invited firms to bid on making parachute cord out of the newly invented fiber—nylon. Western was awarded an initial $200,000 contract to make nylon parachute cord and subsequently produced vast amounts of it during the war.

After WWII, Western began to make fly lines. In 1953, it was marketing its Magi-Brand series in level and tapered configurations. Joe Brooks, the famous fisherman, was a spokesman for Western's Magi-Brand lines. Its flagship fly line in 1954 was the Miller's Hollow series. It came in tapered and level line configurations and had a "Tufcote" coating that did not need dressing. The Miller's Hollow line series manufacturing was done under Patent 2,164,296, which had been issued in 1939 for a method of making braided line with a hollow core to enhance flotation. Western also continued to market its Magi-Braid nylon line. Magi-Braid lines were sold to line distributors for between $10.00 and $15.00 in double tapered and shooting taper configurations. They also sold for between $3.25 and $5.00 for level lines.

MILLER'S HOLLOW FLY LINE
Courtesy of Western Filament, Inc.

By 1960, the firm was making the W-40 nylon floating double taper and level line series, again with a "Tufcote" aerated layer surrounding a braided core. These lines sold to distributors for $9.00 for tapered lines and $2.50 for level lines. Western also produced its W-40 Dacron sinking line series, again with a "Tufcoate" finish.

In marketing its lines, Western developed a popular campaign about *How to catch a Mermaid* that came in booklet form. These were humorous stories that brought a lot of attention to Western's fly lines.

Western was purchased in 1965 by International Fastener Research Corporation, a Los Angeles, CA holding company. This transaction resulted in the firm being renamed West-

WESTERN'S W-40 LOGO
Courtesy of Western Filament, Inc.

ern Filament, Inc. After the acquisition, it was decided to diversify the firm and also focus on industrial products. The diversification did not go smoothly. During the 1970s, Western stopped making many fishing products—including fly lines. Burke Wright became president in 1973 and subsequently purchased the firm in 1978. In 1990, the firm moved to Grand Junction, Colorado (CO). Today, Western focuses on industrial products such as braided sleeves for wiring in airplanes and cars. Western still makes a wide variety of fishing lines including: braided line (4% stretch which allows more powerful hook sets as contrasted to monofilament), Spectra lines (3% stretch), ice fishing line and braided backing.[54]

In 1993, Wayne Wright, Burke Wright's son, became president. Western's Colorado manufacturing facility has over 2000 braiding machines and over 50,000 square feet of manufacturing space. It also has a very complete website showing the full range of its products at www.westernfilament.com.

WESTERN'S HOW TO CATCH A MERMAID
Courtesy of Western Filament, Inc.

SUNSET

Sunset Line and Twine Company (Sunset) was formed in San Francisco, California (CA) in 1932 by Lawrence Christenson and Harry Johnson. The name "Sunset" was selected because of the beautiful sunsets that are seen from San Francisco's Marina District. Christenson and Johnson were in the twine business and the Depression was hurting their business. Thus, they decided to start making linen cuttyhunk fishing lines. Art Agnew, who over time became the controlling stockholder of Sunset, joined the firm as a junior bookkeeper upon his graduation from college in 1935. Art's two sons (Art, Jr. and John) later joined the firm and now have been with the firm for over 35 years.[55]

SUNSET'S ARROWHEAD NYLON FLY LINE

Sunset started making braided silk fly lines in the mid-1930s. Some lines like the TUG-A-WAR Series were enamel-coated and others received a multi-step linseed oil waterproofing treatment. Sometimes it would take 10-11 linseed coats (that were each brushed on and then off) before a line was deemed ready to be sold. Sunset first made level silk lines and then expanded to tapered silk lines. By 1937, Sunset was actively marketing its flagship Arrowhead silk line series.

Sunset enjoyed two advantages pre-WWII. One was that it was the only significant fly line manufacturing firm in the West. The second was that it was very close to San Francisco's Golden Gate Angling & Casting Club (GGACC). The GGACC was a spin off from the San Francisco Fly Casting Club, which had been formed in 1894 and today it is the second oldest club of its type in the U.S. The GGACC has a major casting complex in the heart of San Francisco's Golden Gate Park that was built in 1938 by the Works Project Administration. The GGACC casting pools have been used for many national and international casting tournaments. Many of the West Coast's premiere fly casters were GGACC members (Myron Gregory, Jimmy Green, Jon Tarintino, and so forth) and they worked at the club on new theories about fly line tapers and construction. Jimmy Green also worked at Sunset circa 1954 making fly lines. Thus, Sunset had a ready stream of these world class fly casters coming to it for materials for their new designs. Sunset was able to take advantage of all these experts' experiments in the development of Sunset's new line designs.

In 1940, Sunset moved their manufacturing operations to Petaluma, CA, which is located just north of San Francisco. It has been in the same building ever since. Sunset's building also housed a firm that made silk thread. Sunset was able to buy silk thread for its lines directly from them.

AERIAL PHOTO OF SUNSET BUILDING
Courtesy of Sunset Line and Twine Company

SUNSET'S *FIELD & STREAM* 1943 AD

During WWII, Sunset made parachute cord, lines for emergency kits and a limited amount of fishing lines. They placed ads in magazines such as the May, 1943 *Field & Stream* magazine saying, "Sunset Lines Are in the War!"

In 1953, Sunset opened a second plant in Alabama to make fishing lines. Fly lines were not made at the Alabama plant, which operated until 1969. In California, Sunset and the GGACC developed the first shooting head lines, which were needed for fishing on the big rivers in the West. In fact, Sunset registered the name Shooting Head as a trade name.

Sunset made fly lines both under its own brand and for others (e.g., J. C. Higgins, Montgomery Ward, and Western Auto). Sunset's original silk Arrowhead series was subsequently made in nylon and by 1952, it was also marketing another nylon line series called Stream King. In order to participate in the popular spin casting craze, Sunset (by 1954) was also marketing a 14 foot fly line that could be used with a spinning rod. It was called Taper for Spinning.

SUNSET SPIN-A-FLY LINE

Other fly lines soon appeared such as the Light Cahill series which Sunset was marketing in 1967. Gradually though, Sunset began to de-emphasize fly lines and quit making them by the early 1980s. Sunset's energies became focused on manufacturing other types of fishing lines. It invented and trademarked

Amnesia monofilament, which has virtually no memory and thus lays out straight. In Europe, Amnesia is used today for fishing line and in the United States, it is generally used for backing with shooting head fly lines.

Sunset's Art Agnew also made other significant contributions to the sport of fly fishing. During the 1950s and early 1960s, he was Chairman of the American Fishing Tackle Manufacturers Association (AFTMA's) Special Line Committee. This AFTMA committee worked with Myron Gregory of National Association of Angling & Casting Clubs–U.S. (NAACC) on the new numbered fly line classifications based on line weight. San Francisco's Myron Gregory (champion distance caster) had sponsored a 1957 NAACC resolution to develop new fly line standards. Art Agnew and Myron Gregory worked tirelessly together to develop and implement the new fly line standards which were first adopted by the AFTMA in 1960. These new standards were a watershed event in the history of fly lines.

SUNSET LINE AT THE TIME OF THE NEW AFTMA STANDARDS

ART AGNEW
(Art Agnew turned 90 in 2002.)

Historic line firms that are "gone but not forgotten." These firms were major line manufacturers at one time.

> **Hall Line Corporation (1840)**
> **Rain-Beau (1866)**
> **Weber (c. 1900)**
> **Bevin Wilcox (1919)**
> **Norwich Line Company—S. A. Jones Line Company (1930)**

HALL LINE CORPORATION

Henry Hall was born in 1821 into a Belfast, Ireland family of Irish flax spinners. He came to New York in 1837 and continued his trade of making lines. In 1840, he moved to Highland Mills, NY and formed what became the Hall Line Corporation (Hall Line). As with his line-making competitors of the time, Henry Hall started with an outdoor "line walk" to make lines. Over time, the "line walk" was moved inside a building. The first plant was built at Woodbury Falls, NY, but it was soon moved about 1/2 mile to Highland Mills, NY. At the 100 year mark of Hall Line in 1940, the firm had seen Henry Hall, his son, grandson and great grandson succeeding each other in the firm.

Hall Line made a wide variety of fishing lines out of a wide range of materials (e.g., silk, cotton, Irish linen yarn, Irish flax, and so forth). The word "Celebrated" was used as a brand name from the beginning of the firm and as such, it was an integral part of the firm's early line labels. One of its salesmen's kits from c. 1940 gives one an idea of the wide range of lines that Hall Line made.

Hall Line did not introduce silk fly lines until 1940. Its flagship "Celebrated" fly lines (both level and double tapered configurations) had an oil-fabrication and enameled coating to waterproof them.

During WWII, the Highland Mills plant made parachute cord and line for airmen survivor kits. By 1947, it was marketing its Lake Queen nylon lines in both double tapered and level configurations.

Hall Line closed in the 1960s and a Hall family descendent was its last employee—

HALL SALES KIT (c. 1940)

The HALL Line of FAME

MORE than a century of expert line making is back of every HALL OF FAME line. The same sturdy, dependable quality that today means so much to our men overseas (in Emergency Kits, Parachute Cords and Sutures) is embodied in every yard—whether for fresh or salt water fishing.

Several special processes, exclusive to the HALL OF FAME LINES, in the hands of operators of years and years of experience, produce lines of incomparable smoothness and of just the right absorption to insure maximum strength.

HALL'S CELEBRATED BASS TARPON and TUNA LINE has made tournament history for over 100 years. It is made of top grade pure 50's lea Irish linen yarn. It will stand the toughest abuse, retain its firm twist and will not waterlog.

HENRY HALL founder of the **HALL LINE OF FAME**

Born in a family of flax spinners in Belfast, Ireland, it was natural that upon coming to America, Henry Hall should apply that heritage of skill to the making of fishing lines. Since 1840, through several generations, the same pride of workmanship had made the HALL LINES OF FAME outstanding in popularity.

Many Hall Lines are still at War.

So you may not always be able to secure just the line you want—but the day is not far off, we hope, when dealers everywhere will again have a complete assortment.

Ask Your Dealer

and if you would like our catalog showing the various lines made, drop us a post card or letter. It's yours FREE FOR THE ASKING.

HALL Line CORPORATION
155 PARK AVE. HIGHLAND MILLS, N.Y.

HENRY HALL AND HALL LINE CORPORATION (c. WWII)

Jerome Stanfield, whose aunt was married to Captain A. G. Hall. Of note is that Jerome Stanfield's son (Walt) is married to the daughter (Janice) of the great rod maker, James Payne.[56]

HALL'S FLY LINE

HALL'S WOODBURY FALLS
SILK CASTING LINE

RAIN-BEAU

Canton, Massachusetts was the home of Rain-Beau lines, whose roots trace back to 1821 when Simeon Presbrey began to manufacture twine and thread. William Mansfield subsequently purchased Presbrey's business in 1849 and manufactured cotton twine and threads that were made into blankets for the Civil War. Shortly after the end of the Civil War, William Mansfield's company was turned over to his son, George, who began to manufacture fishing lines as early as March of 1866.[57]

George Mansfield (Mansfield) used twisted silk that was braided into lines of different weights. The lines were dyed various colors and then coated to make them waterproof. These lines became known as Rain-Beau lines. The process took up to six months for a line to reach its proper final condition. Mansfield also made other more economical lines that were faster to produce.

Mansfield expanded several times and also made fishing rods to complement his fishing line business. In 1933, Mansfield's firm was taken over by the Schindler Company from Canada. Schindler continued to make the Rain-Beau brand of lines as well as manufacturing violin, guitar, mandolin and banjo strings. Schindler then resold the firm in 1944. Subsequent owners included International Braid of Providence, RI and Sealand of Torrington, CT.

Rain-Beau lines were featured in a very "sexy" advertising campaign during the 1940s. These ads utilized beautiful girls in swimming suits to promote the lines.

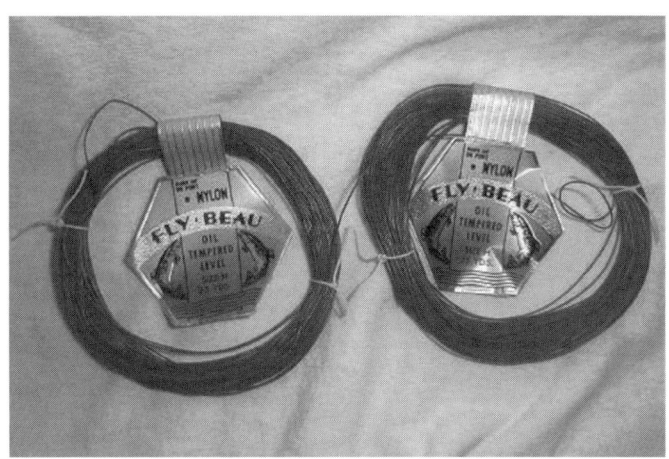

FLY BEAU NYLON LINES

The Hedge 7 Taper line series was developed by Marvin Hedge and patented in 1941 (Patent 2,250,832). Hedge was a well-known fly caster, having won the 1934 American Casting Association national tournament fly rod distance event in St. Louis, Missouri (MO).

SUPER OIL BEAU LINE

HEDGE 7 TAPER LINE

RAIN-BEAU 1946 AD

By 1946, the new owners of Rain-Beau lines were marketing their silk Super Oil Beau fly lines and by 1947 they were marketing their flagship Hedge 7 Taper series. Additionally, they were marketing their nylon Fly-Beau series and their Nyline series of tapered lines.

In 1950, Rain-Beau's owners were marketing their high-end silk Crescent series. Their Super Oil Beau series was their mid-range line that now came in either silk or nylon. Their economical line was the nylon Fly-Beau series. By 1952, Rain-Beau's owners had also developed their silk shooting head "Shooter" series. For the wet fly enthusiasts, a popular series of Dacron Rain-Beau Wet Fly lines was also available.

The manufacturing of Rain-Beau brand lines in Canton, Massachusetts ceased in the late 1950s. Of interest is that the Rain-Beau name still exists on cotton fishing lines made by Can Cord (www.cancord.com), which has since taken over the Schindler Company in Canada. It seems fitting that the Rain-Beau name is still alive today after more than 135 years of lines bearing its proud name.

RAIN-BEAU DACRON WET FLY LINE

WEBER

The genealogy of Weber began with Carrie J. Frost who was born in 1868 in La Crosse, Wisconsin (WI). Her family moved to Stevens Point, WI in 1885. In the early 1890s, she tied some flies for her father and some of his companions. Word quickly spread about her skill in fly tying. Soon, Carrie Frost had developed a fly tying "cottage industry" using local women to make flies. In 1896, her firm (called C. J. Frost Company) emerged from this effort.

In 1920, Carrie Frost sold her firm to a group of local businessmen, who renamed it the Frost Fishing Tackle Company. It then merged with another firm in 1926 to create the Weber Lifelike Fly Company (Weber). Oscar Weber was president and general manager.

Oscar Weber was a very energetic person and soon he was selling a wide range of fishing equipment—not just flies. Oscar Weber was a close friend of Dr. James A. Henshall, a famed angler especially noted for his success with black bass. Dr. Henshall is generally considered to be the first person to design a special rod for use with the newly invented multiplying reel. His recommendations were pub-

CARRIE FROST

OSCAR WEBER
Courtesy of *Wisconsin Sportsman*

WEBER AND FROST BUILDINGS (CIRCA 1920s)
Courtesy of *Wisconsin Sportsman*

lished in 1875 in *Forest & Stream* magazine.[58] Out of Oscar Weber's friendship with Dr. Henshall, a line of Weber fishing equipment was created with Dr. Henshall's name on it.

Weber's 1929 catalog featured the silk Weber's Henshall Vacuum Dressed Fly Casting Line which sold for $3.25-$5.00 for level lines and between $8.00-$10.00 for tapered lines. Our research found no information that Weber made its own fly lines, but there are numerous references about the characteristics Weber wanted in the fly lines it sold. Its fly lines needed to be of a soft finish and were designed to lie straight when cast. Weber encouraged anglers to give fly lines they were considering buying a "floor test" to see if the line lay out on the floor in a straight line or lay out in a corkscrew and twisted manner. Weber felt its lines would win such a test.

All of Weber's growth did not go unnoticed in Stevens Point and by 1940 there were four other firms in the Stevens Point area also making flies. They were the Worth Company, G.W. Frost & Sons (Carrie Frost's brother), Plantico and Marathon Tackle. More than 10 million flies were made annually in the 1940s by these firms. Stevens Point began to be called the "Fly Tying Capital of the World".

WEBER HENSHALL FLY LINE

*WOMEN TYING FLIES FOR WEBER
IN THE LATE 1940s*
Courtesy of *Wisconsin Sportsman*

By 1938, Weber had introduced its Airflow fly line series and by 1940, it had introduced its silk Weber-Henshall Trueflow Taper Fly line. The Trueflow lines were marketed as having better accuracy and casting distance due to the "dynamic-cast" taper of the lines. These lines came in a variety of taper lengths matched both to the weight rod that would be using the line and the type of fishing conditions expected to be encountered.

During WWII, many of the operations at Weber were suspended due to restrictions on key raw materials. Weber did make flies for emergency kits (5,000 dozen per year) as well as other war effort items not associated with sport fishing. Helen Weber, Oscar's daughter, served in the Red Cross for 2 1/2 years during WWII. At one time she held the world's record for Tarpon (length of 5' 10 1/2") caught on a fly rod.

In 1947, Ed Wotruba bought the firm and changed the name from The Weber Lifelike Fly Company to Weber Tackle Company. By 1949, Weber was still marketing its flagship silk Trueflow Taper series ($12.00) as well as its Weber-Henshall silk fly lines in level and tapered configurations. In addition, Weber was selling its Weber Handkraft nylon level lines ($1.50-$2.40) as well as its economical silk Weber Flycaster enameled oil finished level lines, which sold for $1 per 25-yard coil.

By 1957, Weber was marketing a level and tapered nylon series called HI-N-DRI as well as its silk Weber-Henshall Trueflow, and economical Flycaster series. It also marketed its Handkraft level nylon line series. These lines were still being offered in 1960. After 1960, Weber catalogs did not show fly lines.

WEBER SPANISH GUT LEADER

Weber's business suffered after WWII due to Japanese imports (Japan paid 1/10 the hourly wages of U.S. fly tiers.) and from the introduction of the spinning reel.[59] In 1979, the firm was sold again and on March 29, 1985 Weber closed its doors. An auction of the plant equipment and inventory was held in 1988.

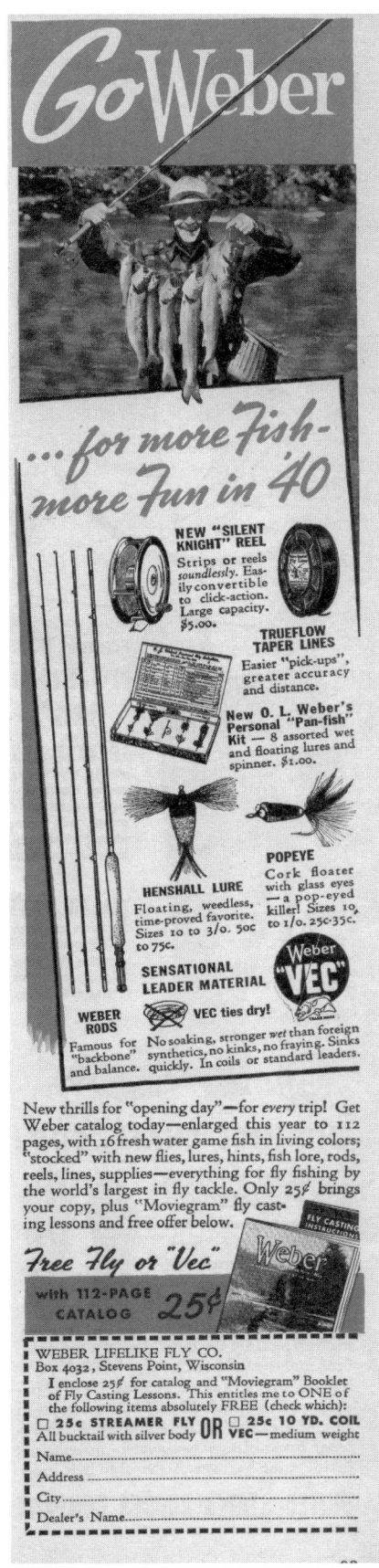

WEBER *OUTDOOR LIFE* 1940 AD

BEVIN WILCOX

Bevin Wilcox Line Company (Bevin Wilcox) was started in 1919 in East Hampton, Connecticut (CT). East Hampton is adjacent to Lake Pocotopaug, which is the largest lake in Connecticut. It is also adjacent to the Salmon and Connecticut Rivers. Bevin Wilcox's founders were Chauncey G. Bevin, Edward L. Wilcox and Mayo S. Purple.[60] Chauncey Bevin was part of the internationally known Bevin family that have been making bells in East Hampton continuously since 1832. Bevin Brothers Manufacturing Company originally made horse sleigh bells and bells for cows and sheep. Most recently they made 20,000 tiny white bells for President Clinton's inauguration that had the presidential seal on them.[61]

Early on, Bevin Wilcox made its lines in a historic saw mill building dating to the 1800s called the Skinner Saw Mill. It made fly lines, waterproofed casting lines and twisted cuttyhunk linen lines for saltwater fishing. Of interest, the firm did very well financially during the Depression as many people had extra time available and began fishing for food.

Bevin Wilcox used the word "Pilot" as the brand name for many of its casting and fly lines. In 1941, it was advertising its Pilot Anglo American soft oil finished fly line as well as its Pilot nylon line series. Bevin Wilcox also had its own brand of fly line dressing called Double Duty, that sold for 25 cents in 1941.

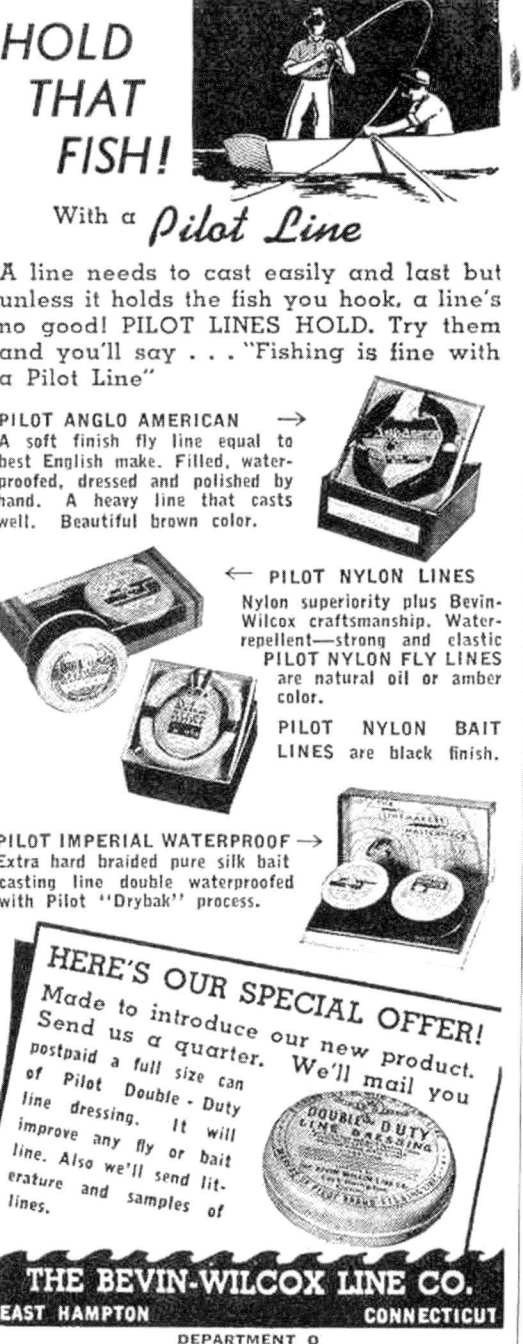

BEVIN WILCOX 1941 AD

BEVIN WILCOX LINE DRESSING

WWII slowed up fishing line production at Bevin Wilcox, but a fisherman could still get certain lines in 1944. The main available fly line was the Pilot oil-dressed fly line series.

BEVIN WILCOX *FIELD & STREAM* 1944 AD

BEVIN WILCOX PILOT LINE

Bevin Wilcox also made a fly line series called Non-Kink that was advertised as being "waterproofed under pressure."

BEVIN WILCOX NON KINK FLY LINE

By the 1960s, Bevin Wilcox's operations in East Hampton were shut down. A few lines were subsequently made in the early 1970's under the Bevin Wilcox label in nearby Moodus, CT by the Brownell Company.[62] Bevin Wilcox was never a large volume manufacturer of fly lines, but it made excellent lines for over four decades.

NORWICH LINE COMPANY—S. A. JONES LINE COMPANY

S. A. (Sam) Jones started a line company in Norwich, New York (NY) in 1930, which was a difficult economic period due to the national depression. In 1935, he sold the business to Frank Zuber, a former mayor of Norwich, NY. It was a small operation as can be seen by the 1938 photo taken of the workers at the plant.

S.A. JONES 1938 STAFF PHOTO
Courtesy of Orrest Karlson, Jr. and Marilyn Neuland

S. A. Jones Line Company made silk fly lines and enameled lines. Like its competitors of the time, its special oil processing techniques were an important selling point to the fishermen. Some lines received up to seven individual oil-processing treatments to ensure their waterproof nature. Its enameled series was called Trout Enameled and its 1938 Governor series was made of "Japan silk."

S.A. JONES 1938 GOVERNOR LINE

S. A. JONES PRESIDENT LINE BALANCED BY MARVIN HEDGE

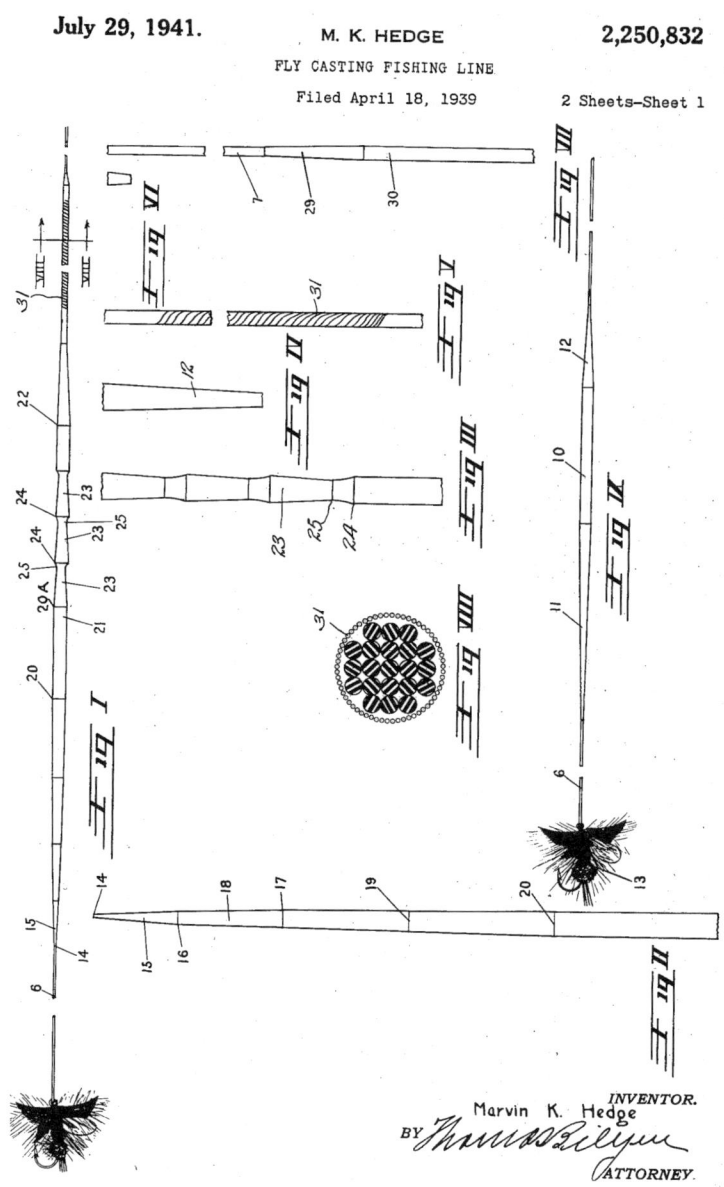

MARVIN HEDGE PATENT

In 1940, Frank Zuber sold the business to J. B. Parsons. During this period, the S. A. Jones Line Company name was dropped in favor of Norwich Line Company (Norwich).

In 1940, Norwich was marketing its "top of the line" Hedge Taper fly line series. Norwich was also making its mid-range Norwich series (oil processed) and economical Trout Haven series (enameled). As part of its marketing program, Norwich adopted the theme "the line of champions." The Norwich Hedge Taper series was named after Marvin Hedge, the famous fly caster from Portland, Oregon. Hedge had introduced the "double haul" to tournament casting in 1934 and had written a popular pamphlet on the technique in 1935. He had been previously sponsored by S. A. Jones Line Company, and would later go on to patent a fly line design in 1941.[63] After WWII, Marvin Hedge worked with Rain-Beau.

Norwich was always active in marketing its lines. In 1940, it had a "Fish of the World" stamp album that included tips on casting by experts. It later invented a plastic utility case to pack its lines, which also could be used for storage of hooks and leaders.

In 1946, Norwich was marketing its Aqua Ranger oil-processed level and tapered fly line series. It also had a Norwich Nylon series that was popular. The Company had dramatically grown under J. B. Parsons' leadership and by 1952 had 600 braiding machines. It was also making a variety of nylon and silk bait casting lines, as well as silk and nylon fly lines.

By the end of the 1950s Norwich went out of business. Its sponsorship of Marvin Hedge and Jimmy Green in international fly casting events such as the 1938 world casting tournament in Paris, France helped establish the U.S. fly fishing industry.[64] Norwich made quality fly lines for three decades that provided significant enjoyment for America's fly fishermen.

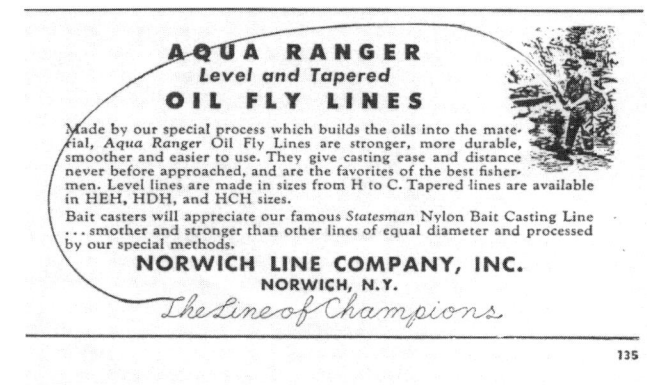

NORWICH *FIELD & STREAM* 1946 AD

NORWICH *FIELD & STREAM* 1940 AD

> **Business combinations/conglomerates (compound line-making genealogy)**
>
> **B. F. Gladding & Company (1816)**
> **Horrocks Ibbotson (c. 1909)**
> **South Bend (1905)**
>
> **Shakespeare (1905)**
> **Pflueger (1886)**
>
> **Cortland (1915)**
> **Newton (1909)**
> **Masterline—U.K. (1970s)**
>
> **Berkley (1937)**
> **Marathon (c. 1937)**
> **Fenwick (1954)**
> **Abu (1921)**
> **Garcia (c. 1920)**
> **Horton Manufacturing Company (Bristol and Kingfisher brands) (1888)**

B. F. GLADDING & COMPANY

Gladding was formed in 1816 in Pharsalia, New York (NY) by John Gladding. He had been an apprentice in a Bristol, Connecticut rope walk and moved his family 300 miles westward to Pharsalia, NY. Upon arrival, John set up a "rope walk" and began making rope. A "rope walk" was where rope strands were laid along a path and then twisted together with the aid of a large wooden wheel. His business was successful and before he died at 46 in 1838, he had turned his business over to his son, James.[65][66]

James Gladding made the first Gladding fishing lines with labor provided by his own family of nine and through the help of 10 neighborhood girls who helped twist lines from cotton and linen. Gradually, fishing lines became a more important product than rope. James' son (B. F. Gladding) subsequently moved the firm to a location on the Otselic River in South Otselic, NY. This new location was just seven miles from its original Pharsalia location. B. F. Gladding renamed the firm B. F. Gladding & Company (Gladding) and installed the company's first braiding machines. These braiding machines were powered by the energy generated by a horse walking in a circular path while connected to wooden sweep device.

It is interesting to note that South Otselic is located in Chenango County, NY and that five major companies ended up making lines within 50 miles of South Otselic. Former New York Governor Rockefeller named South

Otselic "The Fishing Line Capital of the World" in 1966 on the occasion of Gladding's 150th birthday. Gladding noted that the other four competitive firms in the area were either owned or managed by former Gladding employees.

B. F. Gladding dammed up "Old Gladding Gorge" in 1890 and, with the use of waterpower, more mechanical braiders were utilized. In 1897, Gladding introduced an enameling process. It made its first silk lines (Invincible bait casting line) just before 1900.

In the early 1900s, Gladding was in essence the town of South Otselic, which still only had reached a population of 250 in 1949.[67] Gladding's employees also ran the volunteer fire department and the plant's production was curtailed each time there was a fire in the area. After the telephone was invented, people who did not have phones at home went to the plant to use the plant's phones. Local farmers were able to use the plant's machine shops to repair their farm implements.

Life seldom goes perfectly for any family or family-run firm over a 100 year period of time. Keith Angell died in 1938. He was part of the Gladding family and had led the firm from the turn of the century. His death set off a protracted series of lawsuits over future control of the firm that did not end until 1945. Murray Angell, the brother of Keith Angell, became president. His sister-in-law, the widow of Keith Angell (Mrs. Billie Boyce Angell), became Vice President. Billie Angell had started at the plant as a braider tender so she understood the business. In her new role as vice president, she went on to become arguably the most visible woman executive in the line manufacturing industry. With Gladding's new leadership, the firm got past its litigation period and went on to new success.

It should also be noted that Gladding was historically very active in our nation's defense. In the Civil War, when currencies shifted regularly, the Gladding family traded fishing line for food and clothing for the residents of South

GLADDING STAFF PHOTO (CIRCA 1890) IN FRONT OF THE GLADDING PLANT. RALPH BROWN (WITH TIE) ON FAR LEFT IS A GLADDING DECENDENT

Otselic. In WWI, Ralph Brown (a Gladding family member) persuaded the U.S. Government to lift the ban on Gladding using linen, based on the argument that Gladding made three million lines annually. If a fisherman caught ten pounds per year with a single Gladding line then the U.S. would have access to 30 million pounds of fish to help feed its population. In WWII, Gladding made nylon tow ropes for gliders, parachute cord, linings for tank periscopes as well as lines for emergency kits for downed airmen.

It is interesting that Gladding's flagship silk casting and general purpose lines (Invincible and Otselic) did not have Gladding's name on them until 1930. Fishermen had known of these lines for years, but had never heard of Gladding.[68] Gladding began to advertise aggressively their own firm after 1930.

GLADDING 1957 CATALOG

In 1937, the Trans-Lu-Cent line series was Gladding's new flagship silk line and it had a special oil finish to give it a mist or translucent color. Gladding's Maple Leaf was an oil-tempered, mid-range line that was featured as being non-sticking and non-kinking. The Whip Slik was the most economical of these three new silk lines. Gladding also still made Otselic and Invincible silk lines. The Otselic silk line was marketed as an all-around level line that could be used for fly casting, bait casting, trolling, ice fishing or saltwater fishing.

MRS. BILLIE ANGELL (COLEMAN)

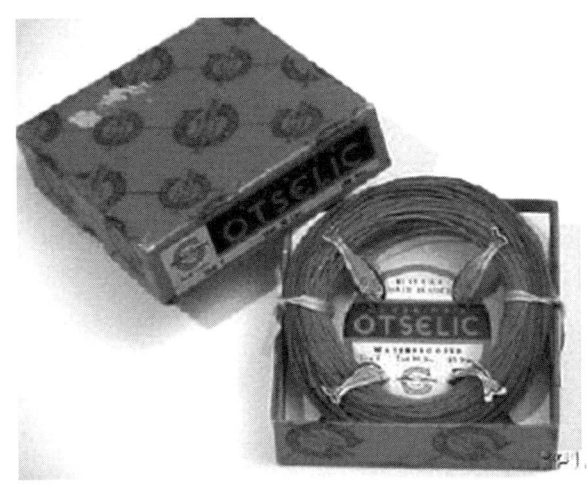

GLADDING OTSELIC LINE

Nylon was invented in 1934 and nylon fishing lines appeared in 1939. Gladding soon had a series of nylon lines to complement its silk fly lines. A 1950 catalog shows the Dauntless nylon fly line and the economical Ripple nylon fly line. The Dauntless line in 25-yard spools sold for $1.92 for a level (size H) line, while a tapered Dauntless (size HEH) line sold for $9.85. In contrast, Ripple lines were level and sold in 25-yard spools for $1.67. Silk lines were still featured in the 1950 Catalog, with the Trans-Lu-Cent series selling for $12.00 for a 30-yard tapered line (size HEH) and the Whip-Slik series selling for $10.95 (size HEH). Gladding also had a Magistrate series of nylon lines as well as a Super line series.

GLADDING RIPPLE NYLON LINES

In 1951, Gladding introduced its new tapered nylon Cilesto series that was Cilestone processed. Gladding was located in S. Otselic, NY and Cilesto was a word created by spelling Otselic in reverse. The Cilestone process was designed to better seal and impregnate the line's nylon threads and to help the line's floating ability.

In 1953, Gladding introduced the famous AEROFLOAT floating line that had gas bubbles sealed into the line. This series continued to be improved and by 1957 was the firm's flagship line. 30-yard tapered (size HEH) lines cost $10.00 in 1957. Gladding also offered the shorter and thus more economical BUB-L-ETT tapered series (45-foot fly line with 75-foot mono-braid backing) containing the Aerofloat technology. A BUB-L-ETT line of size HEH taper cost $4.95.

GLADDING AEROFLOAT FLY LINE

In 1950, L. L. Witherill and Jack Dougherty acquired controlling interest of Gladding after six generations of Gladding family ownership. In 1954, the firm produced the equivalent of over 86,000 miles of fishing lines.

In 1954, Scientific Anglers (SA) developed a method to put a tapered plastic coating on a level braided line. SA filed for patent in 1954 on this new technology and the patent was issued on November 15, 1960. SA had developed the new patent in the same time period that it was providing consulting engineering services to Gladding. The contract between the two firms gave Gladding certain rights to use the invention. Gladding took the position on March 17, 1955 that it had an exclusive right to use the technology and sued SA. Gladding was granted a temporary injunction and SA was forced to stop making fly lines.

Litigation over who could use the patent went back and forth between SA and Gladding until June, 1957—when Gladding finally won. SA was temporarily out of the fly line business, but Gladding had to pay SA a 5% royalty on all lines made using the SA patented technology.

SA then developed a second variable coating method that was not in conflict with the first patent. A SA patent for the second technology was filed in July 1958 and issued in November 1960. Soon after the second patent was issued, an agreement was made in which SA gave Gladding the right to use the second patent technology. In exchange, Gladding gave SA the right to use the first patent technology. Both firms could now use both patents and SA gave up the 5% first patent royalty owed them from Gladding. This arrangement was good for both firms as the first patent technology turned out to be easier to operate than the second patent and now SA could use that technology. Gladding ended up having access to both technologies and no longer owed SA a 5% royalty.

Previously, in 1957, Gladding had featured wet fly lines including the Dacron Aqua-Sink for all-around wet fly and nymph fishing. Additionally, Gladding featured the Steelheader and Salmon tapered lines for deep fly fishing as well as the economical braided nylon Magistrate floating line series ($5.00 for 30-yards of size HEH).

Gladding then went into a rapid growth phase through the purchase of South Bend (1964), Horrocks Ibbotson (1967), Bronson, Payne Rod, two English Companies, K. P. Morritt, Ltd. (Morritt) and Edgar Sealey and Sons, Ltd. Morritt was known for their fishing reels and for their "Octopus" fishing hooks. Gladding also diversified into non-fishing businesses such as sports and hunting clothes, recreational vehicles, flotation products, sleeping bags, bowling bags, toboggans, home stereos, water skis, and so forth.[69]

Several notable new line series came out of all of this business expansion. The acquisition of Payne Rod resulted in a Payne line series, which is highly desirable by fly line collectors. Jim Payne was a major rod supplier to Abercrombie & Fitch and Gladding also made lines for them.

GLADDING PAYNE FLY LINE

Unfortunately, all this expansion proved hard to manage and Gladding ended up declaring bankruptcy. Gladding made fishing lines and other fishing equipment during most of America's history which resulted in countless hours of pleasure for countless Americans.

Note: The Gladding name is not totally gone today. Wellington Leisure Products of Madison, Georgia sells a Gladding twine series—see www.wellingtoninc.com.

HORROCKS IBBOTSON

Horrocks Ibbotson (HI) of Utica, New York traces it roots back to a small store operated by George Austin during the War of 1812. His nephew, George Austin Clark, hired H. J. Horrocks (Horrocks) as a clerk in the store in 1863. George Austin Clark and Horrocks then formed a company called Clark Horrocks, in about 1900. Of interest is that Horrocks had previously acquired the fishing rod company of George Camp in 1890.[70][71]

E. D. Ibbotson became associated with Horrocks in about 1896, and in 1909 they formed HI. Many more acquisitions were to follow including: Abbey & Imbrie in 1931. Abbey & Imbrie was the fishing tackle division of the Spalding Company—their oldest competitor. In the years before WWII, HI became one of the largest split cane rod makers in the U.S.

HI had a longstanding role in line manufacturing as well as manufacturing other types of fishing equipment. They advertised themselves as "Manufacturers of the largest line of fishing equipment in the world." In addition to its own line manufacturing, HI controlled American Line Company of Utica, NY (E. D. Ibbotson was president of both firms in 1931.) American Line Company was an innovative line manufacturer and developed a plastic coated fishing line in 1942, called Flex. This line was sold as a casting and a fly line.

AMERICAN LINE FLEX SERIES

Prior to WWII, HI marketed their Old Gold fly line, which was a reasonably priced premium silk fly line (a level line sold for $1.75 in 1940). It also sold other silk fly lines including the Supreme series (a high-end line that sold for $8.00 in 1938), and the Para Shoot series (a line that sold for $5.00 in 1941).

HI OLD GOLD LINE

In addition to making lines and other sport fishing equipment, HI always helped fisherman better understand how to use its products. Its spokesman was "Old Hi" (a pipe-smoking fictionalized character) who had a wealth of knowledge about fishing. There were fishing guides such as "Old Hi's Fresh and Saltwater Fishing Guide." Old Hi also gave tips on how to install fly lines easily onto fly reels.

ery budget including:

- Dry Flite (an oil-tempered nylon tapered line which sold for $8.00)
- Defiance (a medium-priced, single-tapered, nylon line which sold for $4.45)
- Ambassador (a level, oiled nylon line which sold for $1.30-$2.20)
- National Sportsman (a level line which sold for $1.00-$1.65)
- Rainbow (an enameled line selling for 75-85 cents).

1954 HI CATALOG FEATURING "OLD Hi"

HI RAINBOW ENAMELED SILK LINE

After WWII, HI greatly expanded its number of fly lines. It created a wide range of fly lines including the new Float series, a vinyl coated nylon line with a hollow center to insure floating. HI received its nylon directly from DuPont and then extruded its own monofilament. A Float line (size HDH) cost $8.50 in 1954. In addition to the new Float series was the venerable Old Gold silk series. It sold in 1954 for $8.50 for a size HEH line and $2.00 for a level size H line. In 1954, there were also a number of other fly lines to match ev-

Of interest, HI was also importing and selling the Milwards' tapered lines from England at a cost of $16.80 for size HDH line. Clearly, high-end American lines were very cost competitive with these English lines.

By 1955, HI published its 45th edition catalog and to its credit began to introduce environmental themes in the catalog. This catalog said on its cover, "Fight Pollution—For Better Health and Better Fishing", which is still true today.

Richard Balch (a grandson of H. J. Horrocks) who had been with the firm since 1922 and president since 1942, purchased the company in 1960. Myron Ibbotson then ended his association with HI.

In 1967, the Gladding Corporation bought HI and put it into its ever-expanding conglomerate of fishing and recreational product companies. HI moved all of its 1,500 braiding machines to Gladding, which could make lines that cost less because Gladding was not unionized. Gladding would later go bankrupt.

HI was a major force in line manufacturing for many decades. It always made a highly functional series of fly lines and sold them at fair price.

SOUTH BEND

The Worden Bucktail Manufacturing Company began in 1905 in South Bend, Indiana (IN). Frank G. Worden (Bucktail Worden) had invented bucktail fishing lures in his kitchen and went into business making and selling them. By 1909, the firm had changed its name to the South Bend Bait Company (South Bend). In the early stages of the firm, the ownership changed numerous times. Ivar Hennings became manager of the Company in 1911. Hennings, after becoming president in about 1915, led the firm from having sales of $7,000 per year in 1911 to having annual sales of over a million dollars in 1926. By 1927, South Bend was making split cane and steel rods and selling its Bass Oreno lure, which at that time was the most widely used lure in the world. In the 1920s, South Bend purchased the Cross Rod and Tackle Company and moved it to South Bend, IN.

The firm's 1936 statistics (with Ivar Hennings still at the helm) showed how much South Bend had grown. It sold 4,000,000 yards of silk casting line, 664,553 bait casting lures, 620,998 fly rod lures, 141,696 reels and was making 2,000 split cane rods per week of which 75% were fly rods. Clearly, South Bend was a major force in the fishing equipment market place.

IVAR HENNINGS

Our research has not been able to show that prior to WWII that South Bend made any significant portion of the fly lines it sold. Apparently, South Bend had fly lines made to its specifications by other firms. Right after WWII, South Bend purchased an interest in Soo Valley Lines (Soo Valley) in Esterville, Iowa for the production of braided lines.[72] Shakespeare was the other owner of Soo Valley. We also know that both Cortland and Scientific Anglers made lines at various times for South Bend.[73][74] Many fly fishermen bought and used South Bend fly lines both before and after WWII. South Bend always sold a wide range of other fishing lines that met every customer's pocketbook. For example, for cane pole fisherman, it sold the inexpensive Pole-Oreno line.

SOUTH BEND EXCEL ORENO SILK LINE

SOUTH BEND POLE ORENO LINE

The trade name "Oreno" is common to many South Bend products. A 1929 newspaper article said the name was selected as follows: "Ivar Hennings was looking for the name of a certain bass bait some years ago and remarked: 'Well, isn't it too bad not to be able to think of a name for such a peachorino.' "[75] The marketing light then came on and soon there were Cast-orenos, Trout-orenos, Fly-orenos, and so forth.

South Bend fly lines also used the word "Oreno" extensively. In the mid-1930s the Excel Oreno appeared and became South Bend's flagship silk line. A circa 1935 line, the Excel Oreno, was made of "Pure Japan Silk" and was also oil processed. In 1937, South Bend marketed a Chief Oreno. In 1938, it was marketing a Fish Oreno, and in 1940 it was marketing a Trout Oreno.

SOUTH BEND FISH ORENO SILK LINE

SOUTH BEND TROUT ORENO LINE

As previously mentioned, there was a South Bend fly line priced for every budget. For example, in 1940, a Trout Oreno silk level line cost $1.50 for a 25-yard length. A double tapered Fish Oreno cost $2.50 for a 25-yard length. Finally, a level Excel Oreno cost $3.00 and a double tapered Excel Oreno cost $9.00 for 25 and 30-yard lengths, respectively.

With the start of WWII, South Bend began to convert to military production. The War Production Board required tackle manufacturers to discontinue the use of critical materials like plastic, brass, steel and cork by May 31, 1942. South Bend was able to "moth ball" its machinery for making split cane rods, but the remainder of its operations was revamped for the production of war goods.

When the war was over, South Bend converted back to making fishing equipment. Conversion back to full pre-war production levels was slow in occurring due to the shortage of critical materials. South Bend developed a small brochure, which had a collection of fishing contest photos. This brochure was sent back to customers who had inquired about new fishing equipment which just was not available yet. It did not get the customer the equipment they wanted, but clearly showed that South Bend cared.

SOUTH BEND BROCHURE (POST-WWII)

SOUTH BEND MEMO SENT ALONG WITH "FISHING PHOTOS"

By 1948, nylon had become popular and the flagship Excel Oreno name was now being used on nylon fly lines. Line prices had stayed roughly the same between 1940 and 1948 with a 1948 level nylon Excel Oreno costing between $1.85 and $3.00 and the tapered series costing $9.00.

The Company changed its name to South Bend Tackle Company in 1955. In late 1964, Gladding Corporation purchased South Bend. At the time of the acquisition, South Bend was marketing its Banshee floating fly lines that did not need dressing ($5.00 for level and $10.00 for tapered lines) and its Super-Jet floating fly line series ($3.35 for level and $6.75 for tapered lines). Later, the Gladding Corporation would go bankrupt.

South Bend products always were a good value for their cost. The prices of its fly lines had a wide cost range and thus allowed its customers to select a fly line that they could afford. South Bend was clearly an American institution that outfitted countless fly fishermen.

Note: The name South Bend lives on. In 1981, two Chicago families resurrected the South Bend name and began selling sport fishing equipment again. They have a web site at www.south-bend.com.

SHAKESPEARE

William Shakespeare, Jr. of Kalamazoo, Michigan developed and obtained a patent in 1896 for a device to wind line evenly on a spool when retrieving a lure with a fishing reel. This invention led to the formation of the William Shakespeare, Jr. Corporation in 1905. In addition to selling fishing equipment, the firm also marketed tennis rackets, baseball equipment, watches, and so forth. In 1915, the firm changed its name to the Shakespeare Company (Shakespeare).

WILLIAM SHAKESPEARE IN 1924
Courtesy of Shakespeare Fishing Tackle

During WWI, the firm manufactured mortar fuses. During WWII, Shakespeare had contracts for the construction of controls for aircraft, tanks, jeeps and the Norden bombsight. Shakespeare has had a long history of making fly lines as well as using the associated manufacturing techniques (braiding, weaving, twisting, and so forth) in other non-fishing related endeavors. In 1921, it diversified into automotive products—such as cables using twisted wires.

Shakespeare made lines early on in their Michigan manufacturing operations. For instance, they advertised in 1951 that they had been making lines for half-a-century. Some of its late 1930s lines were named with Michigan historical terminology, such as their Cadillac series, an enameled "super-silk" fly line. Other popular silk fly lines were Shakespeare's Majestic series made of "super-silk" and their Tru-arT oil finished series.

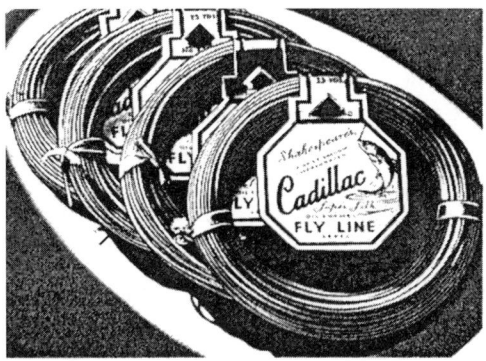

SHAKESPEARE'S CADILLAC SILK FLY LINE

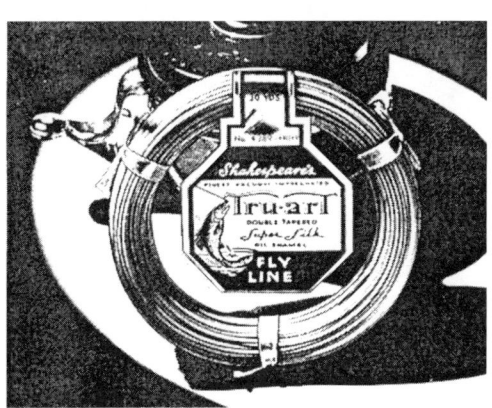

SHAKESPEARE'S TRU ART SILK LINE

By 1940, Shakespeare expanded into nylon line production with its "Nylon" fly line series. In 1946, it moved its Michigan line manufacturing operations to Esterville, Iowa and incorporated as the Soo Valley Company, Inc. (Soo Valley). Shakespeare made fly lines as well as monofilament lines at Soo Valley. Its casting lines were made under the Wexford name.

By 1951, Shakespeare had a wide range of silk and nylon fly lines including:

- Cadillac silk line—a level line that sold for $2.10-$3.55
- Majestic silk line—a double-tapered line that cost $8.50 and a level line that cost $1.70-$3.15
- Tru-arT silk line—a double-tapered line that sold for $11.00
- Au Sable nylon line—a double-tapered line that sold for $7.80 and a level line that sold for $1.50-$2.40
- "Nylon" series line—a double-tapered line that sold for $9.00 and a level line that sold for $1.90-$3.10.

In 1952, Shakespeare developed a nylon line series called Formula 12-0-9, which denoted the line's finish that was developed in conjunction with Dr. Arthur Howald—the inventor of the fiberglass Wonderod.

By 1955, Shakespeare was selling its popular Wonderfloat fly line series. This line series was marketed as "floats without dressing" with the secret being in the "floating jacket."

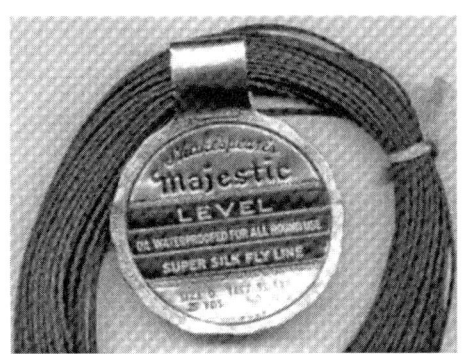

SHAKESPEARE'S MAJESTIC SUPER SILK FLY LINE

SHAKESPEARE WONDERFLOAT LINE

SHAKESPEARE WONDERFLOAT LINE BOX

SHAKESPEARE PURIST LINE

In 1956, Soo Valley moved its operations to Columbia, South Carolina and began to make Polyvinyl Chloride (PVC) plastic coated lines.[76] Its next generation of line coating equipment had two wheels that were grooved and revolved in counterclockwise motions. The wheels were about 3 inches in diameter and when the grooves came together, they worked together to facilitate placement of a tapered PVC (vinyl) coating on the line. Shakespeare would make continuous line in this process (approximately 1,000 yards). The speed of the wheels was such that one full revolution made one complete 30-yard fly line. The wheels were notched to put a "blob" of material on the continuous line to show where one line stopped and the next one began. The continuous line was cut at these "blob" locations to create individual fly lines.

As some of the early developers of PVC coated lines, Shakespeare had new technical problems that it worked hard to overcome. Liquid PVC vinyl was used for the plastic coating on lines. It was very similar to the vinyl material used to make auto seat cushions at the time. The vinyl plasticizers needed to keep the fly lines flexible tended to leach out and then the lines would become brittle. In order to overcome this problem, Shakespeare developed a line cleaning dressing that both cleaned the line and also added back plasticizer. Shakespeare also had to treat the braided nylon inner line to get good coating adhesion, as adhesion to nylon is inherently difficult. When Shakespeare wanted to make floating lines it added microballoons from Minnesota Mining and Manufacturing Co. (3M) similar to the Scientific Anglers' process. Finally, when Shakespeare wanted sinking lines, it added clay or fine solid glass particles.

Shakespeare made lines under its own label. Additionally, it sold bulk lines to others for rebranding—Sears was also a major customer. Ted Williams was active in some of the Shakespeare-Sears line designs along with Ben Hardisty. Hardisty was a champion fisherman who first became a Shakespeare salesman and then a Shakespeare executive.

When the new AFTMA line standards were introduced in the early 1960s, Shakespeare was marketing its Wonderfloat, Executive, Wexfloat, Presidential and Purist series.

SHAKESPEARE WEXFLOAT FLY LINE

SHAKESPEARE EXECUTIVE LINE

SHAKESPEARE PRESIDENTIAL FLY LINE

In 1965, Shakespeare acquired the interests of Topp Tackle, which included the former Allcock and Young's manufacturing operations in Redditch, England. The origins of these facilities dated back as far as 1880 and made them one of the England's oldest and largest manufacturers of fishing tackle. The town of Redditch has long been regarded as the center of the British fishing tackle industry.

In 1966, Shakespeare acquired the Pflueger Corporation of Akron, Ohio. This united two of the world's oldest names in the fishing tackle industry. In 1979, Anthony Industries (Anthony) of Los Angeles, CA bought 35% of Shakespeare. The South Carolina based Shakespeare line-making operations were moved to England in the late 1980s. Today, Shakespeare is still producing lines in the U.K.

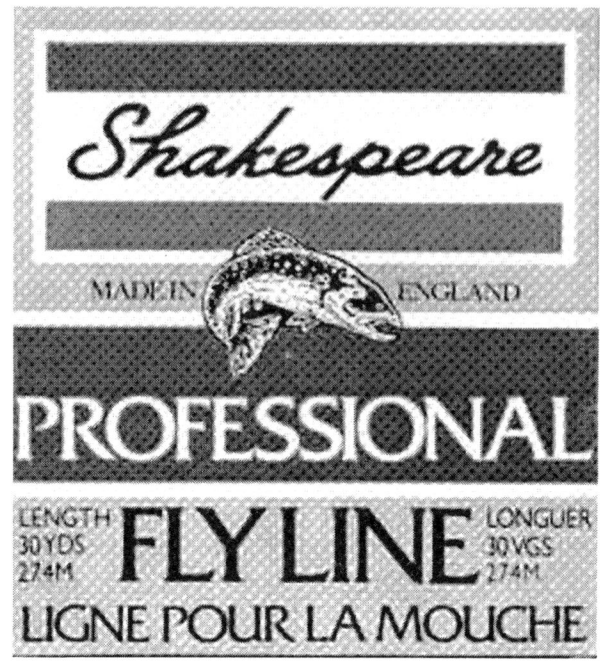

SHAKESPEARE LINE MADE IN ENGLAND

In 1996, Shakespeare's ownership established a new corporate identity as Anthony changed its name to K2, Inc. Shakespeare has a comprehensive web site at www.shakespeare-fishing.com, which provides information on all its products. There is a sister web site for Shakespeare-U.K., which is www.shakespeare-fishing.co.uk.

PFLUEGER

Pflueger was started by Ernest F. Pflueger, a native of Baden, Germany. He was orphaned in Germany and came to America to live with his brother and sister in Buffalo, New York. Pflueger was an inventor of a wide number of items including fishing tackle and illuminated bait and he obtained 50 patents. He moved to Akron, Ohio and started a company (Enterprise Works) in 1881 to manufacture his inventions. In 1886, with the help of several people (including Dr. B. F. Goodrich of tire making fame), he incorporated the Enterprise Manufacturing Company (Enterprise). In the same year, Enterprise acquired the American Fish Hook Company, which had been established in 1864. Ernest F. Plfueger's son, Ernest Andrew Pflueger, also formed a fishing tackle company, which was consolidated into Enterprise in 1913. Ernest Andrew Pflueger was president of Enterprise from 1913-42 and was followed by his son, John, as executive vice president in 1942 and president in 1950. Charles T. Pflueger, Sr. and Jr. also worked in the firm as did William S. Pflueger. Other Pflueger family members followed—it was a family run operation.[77]

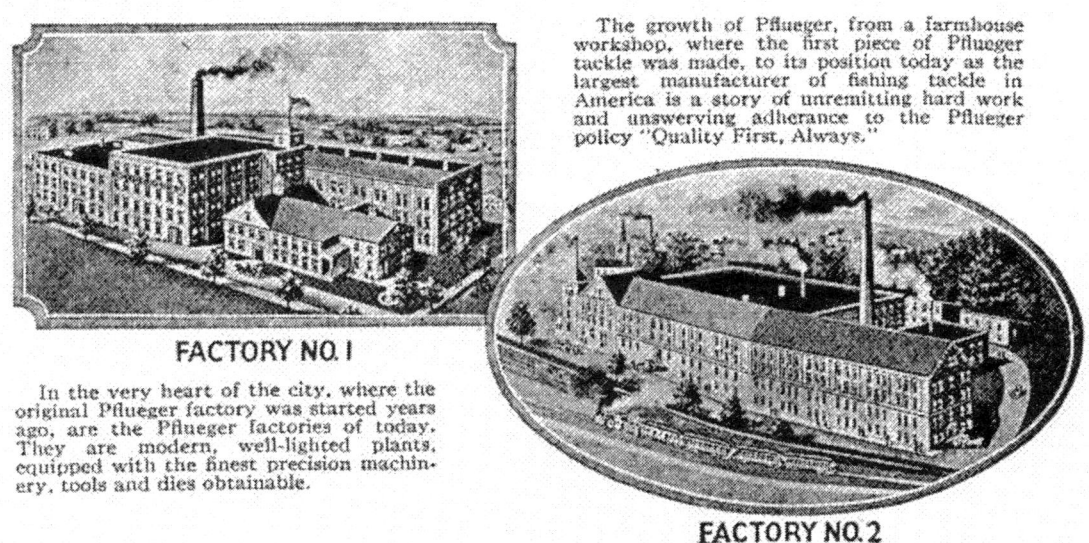

PFLUEGER PLANT 1 AND 2 PHOTO (C. 1934)

Enterprise grew rapidly. The Pflueger Supreme reel was introduced in 1916 and instantly became an American institution. One employee, Louis Valentine, had personally assembled over 500,000 Supreme reels before he retired in 1958—after 52 years with the Company. The company also introduced the famous Medalist fly reel. It is the rare fly fisherman that has not owned at least one Medalist fly reel.

Our research has not been able to show that Pflueger made any significant portion of the fly lines it sold. Apparently, it had fly lines made to their specifications by other firms. This is not surprising given the fact that it was selling 3,000 different items of fishing tackle through 32,000 dealers and 1,000 distributors by 1954. Due to its huge market presence, many fly fishermen bought and used Pflueger fly lines.

One fly line that was sold extensively was the NEVERSINK silk line.

PFLUEGER NEVERSINK LINE

When nylon came into common usage, Pflueger began to market its Oriole Nylon line, which was Vacuoil-processed.

PFLUEGER ORIOLE NYLON LINE AND BOX

In 1966, Pflueger was purchased by the Shakespeare Company. Ben Hardesty was selected by Shakespeare to head Pflueger. Shakespeare had a long history of line manufacturing and soon the two merged firms were manufacturing and marketing lines under both the Pflueger and Shakespeare labels. Shakespeare catalogs often show Shakespeare fly lines in one section and Pflueger fly lines in another section of the same catalog.

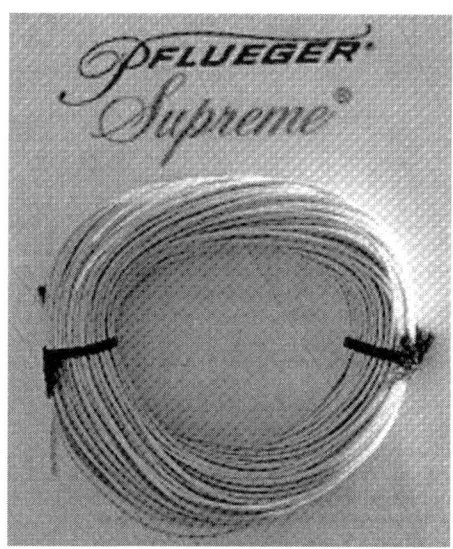

PFLUEGER SUPREME LINE

The fly line operations of Shakespeare and Pflueger subsequently were moved to England. The Pflueger name still has a great deal of recognition and respect in the market place and English Pflueger lines are periodically seen in the U.S.

In 1979, Anthony Industries (Anthony) of Los Angeles, CA bought 35% of Shakespeare (which now included Pflueger). Shakespeare's ownership got a new corporate identity in 1996 when Anthony changed their name to K2, Inc.

CORTLAND

The Cortland Line Company (Cortland) started in Cortland, New York (NY), in 1915, when Ray F. Smith acquired a few braiding machines and began manufacturing braided silk bait casting lines. Ray Smith had previously owned and operated a clothing store in Cortland, NY. During WWI, Cortland switched from making fishing lines to making surgical sutures for the war effort.

RAY SMITH
Courtesy of Cortland Line Company

Following WWI, Cortland grew rapidly. Ironically, the Depression period of 1932-1936 helped Cortland. Many people without jobs and with time on their hands turned to fishing for recreation and food. Cortland had a wide range of fly lines by 1932, which included the economical Fair Play series and the Native Trout and Say Brook enameled silk line series. Cortland's line business boomed at the same time America's economy was in the doldrums.

By 1941, Cortland's business was organized into three divisions. The Line Division made a wide variety of fishing lines; the Narrow Fabrics Division made shoelaces and corset laces; and the Tennis Racket Division made laminated wooden tennis rackets. Wilson Sporting Goods acquired the Tennis Racket Division c. 1960 and built a new plant in Cortland, NY to make rackets. About a decade later, Wilson closed its plant and Cortland repurchased it and remodeled it into their current manufacturing facility.

Cortland manufactured a wide variety of enameled silk and oil-impregnated fly lines during its early years. Most of the lines were made for others, but some had the Cortland label. Cortland's lines included the Say Brook enameled silk series, the Bumble Bee series, the Regal Scot series and the "top of the line" Ivanhoe oil-impregnated silk fly line series.

CORTLAND SAY BROOK LINE

CORTLAND REGAL SCOT LINE

CORTLAND FAIR PLAY LINE

CORTLAND IVANHOE SILK LINE

Most of Cortland's competitors started making their silk lines by using silk thread made by others. Cortland, on the other hand, started with raw silk in block form from the silk cocoons. The silk filaments were taken off the block of silk and then combined into strands of thread, which could then be braided into a fly line. The process of braiding tapered fly lines was very labor intensive. An employee could only make one line per shift per braiding machine and the same employee could only operate eight machines at a time. This meant that a braiding machine employee's total output was only eight tapered lines per shift. The slow line production rate was due to the need to add or remove threads in order to make the taper in the line.

Following the manufacturing of a tapered silk line, the line was put through a waterproofing process in which linseed and tongue oils were impregnated into the line. This impregnation process utilized a three story high building. The lines were first impregnated with the linseed and tongue oil mixture in a vat on the first story. They were then stretched upward to the third story where they went over a pulley and then back to the impregnation vat on the first story. In the second story, the impregnated lines were heated and excess material was taken off by running the lines through a circular orifice die. This process was repeated over and over until the line had received the proper waterproofing.

When WWII came, Cortland converted to making parachute and bomb cords. When the war was over, Cortland faced a pent-up demand caused by the soldiers and civilians wanting to get back to sport fishing. This period also saw a change in Cortland's sales policy from being primarily a private brand manufacturing firm (e.g., making lines for Montgomery Ward, South Bend, Western Auto, and so forth) to beginning to sell more lines under its own label.

In 1948, Cortland introduced its nylon Cam-O-Flage series of bait casting lines and fly lines. Previous fly lines had generally been solid colored and the new Cam-O-Flage lines were based on WWII camouflaging techniques. Cam-O-Flage line color changed every foot or so and helped the line to be less visible in the water. This concept was very popular with the public as they had seen first hand the advantages of camouflaging during the war. Other line manufacturers soon followed with their camouflaged sequels, but Cortland had copyrighted the name Cam-O-Flage and remained the industry leader in this popular type of lines.

CORTLAND CAM-O-FLAGE LINE

In 1952, Cortland technicians discovered it was possible to apply a vinyl coating over a braided and tapered nylon core line. The line floated because the coating was impervious to water and the air trapped in the braided core allowed it to float. This new line was originally shown to the public at a sportsman's show in Milwaukee, Wisconsin in the spring of 1952. The centerpiece of those sportsman's shows was a large water tank. During the show, this tank would be used for casting exhibitions, retrieving dog exhibitions, and so forth. Cortland's Leon Chandler was their sales representative at the Milwaukee show and he simply put the light green prototype fly line in the water and let it float for hours. No one had ever seen a line float for hours without dressing and the line became a sensation. Leon was repeatedly asked for the name of the line and just "pulled the name X333 out of the air." His sales-driven idea was that X333 connoted a line made by countless experiments. Upon returning to Cortland, management officially had to name the line and, after much discussion, they decided to reaffirm Leon's 333 name. They also had to decide what color to use for the line and again they decided to stay with the light green color of the prototype. The 333 was an instant success and Cortland's entire 1953 season's production sold out within a few weeks. Cortland continued to make the 333, using their technology, through the end of the 1950s.[78]

CORTLAND 333
Courtesy of Cortland Line Company

In parallel with Cortland's line research that made the 333 line truly float, Scientific Anglers (SA) was approaching the same line flotation challenge in a different way. SA developed a means to put a tapered plastic coating over a level braided core and fill that coating with microscopic hollow spheres to make the line float. SA patented its approach, which proved to be the superior one of the two methods. Cortland and SA then made a licensing agreement so that Cortland could have access to SA's technology. In c. 1962, Cortland received SA's first tapered coating machines and began manufacturing its lines under SA's technology. Cortland continued to develop its own technology for line-making which was subsequently utilized in 1972.

Many skilled employees were needed for all of Cortland's growth. Ray Smith had a knack for selecting outstanding employees. He hired John Dittenheffer in 1929 to run the financial end of Cortland—which he did for decades. In 1941, he hired E. P. "Pete" Hoyle as vice president of sales and also hired young Leon Chandler to work in the accounting department. Hoyle was an experienced veteran in the fishing equipment business having previously been employed at Richardson Rod and Reel Company and Horton-Bristol Manufac-

1953 LINE GUIDE AND FORECASTER—"333 WAS NEW FOR 53"

turing Company. His leadership was important in the post-WWII growth era for Cortland and he eventually became president of Cortland. As an indication of the industry respect for Pete Hoyle, upon his death he was posthumously inducted into the American Fishing Tackle Manufacturers Association (AFTMA's) Fresh Water Hall of Fame.

Pete Hoyle recognized the talent Leon Chandler brought to the organization and helped Leon move from accounting to sales. Leon Chandler would go on to be the individual the public most identified as Cortland since he worked in external roles for Cortland for over 50 years. In 1959, Leon became part of the AFTMA committee that developed the new weight-based standards for fly lines, which superceded the previous diameter-based standards. Leon subsequently served twice as AFTMA President and once as National President of Trout Unlimited. Over his career, Leon represented Cortland at countless trade shows, seminars, wrote numerous instructional pamphlets, and so forth. In recognition of his 50 years of service to the sport of fly fishing, Leon Chandler was selected as the 1992 Angler of the Year *by Fly Rod & Reel* magazine.

LEON CHANDLER
Courtesy of Leon Chandler

In early 1958, Ray Smith sold Cortland to a small conglomerate owned by Aero Supply Manufacturing Company and Schmeig Industries. The ownership of Cortland changed hands again in 1972 when Jack Murray (president of Cortland since 1963) and a group of local Cortland, NY investors bought Cortland back from the Aero Supply-Schmeig Industries conglomerate. Then, the new owners opened ownership of Cortland up to its employees in 1979. Today, the firm is employee-owned.

Cortland developed a new premium fly line, the 444, during the early 1960s. Its finish was smoother and more supple than the 333 and the 444 line series also had more precise taper configurations. One of the other new characteristics of the 444 series was that all 444 lines were inspected by running the full length of the line through an inspector's fingers to check for imperfections. In 1984, the rejection rate of 444 lines was one out of three, which was an indication of the extremely high quality associated with 444 lines that reached the consumer.[79]

CORTLAND 444 Line

The introduction of the 444 fly line led to the development of the Cortland Certified Fishing Pro Shop Program in 1965. This was a way for Cortland to sell its premium products in specialty fly shops while still being able to sell its 333 lines in discount and general retail stores. This concept was well received and by 1984, there were more than 700 specialty fly shops and stores selling Cortland premium products.

CORTLAND CERTIFIED FISHING PRO SHOP BROCHURE

In 1975, Cortland bought the Fishing Line Division from Newton Line Company (Newton) in nearby Homer, NY. Newton had been in business since 1909 and selling its Fishing Line Division to Cortland allowed Newton to focus on its industrial cordage and filament business. This acquisition brought two monofilament line-extruding machines to Cortland and marked Cortland's entry into the monofilament line market.

Cortland continued to improve its basic 333 and 444 lines. Over time, the venerable 333 was upgraded to the 333HT (High Technology). The 333HT lines had harder and smoother finishes than the earlier 333 series. In 1979, Cortland introduced the 444SL (Specialized Line) series of lines. The genesis for the 444SL lines occurred when Leon Chandler was in Canada fishing with baseball's Ted Williams—an active fly fisherman who knew a lot about fly lines. Williams thought the standard 444 line was too soft for the long casts needed in Canadian waters. Cortland made up some stiffer lines with new taper lengths and found that they did cast farther.

The 444SL taper began at 12 feet for 3-5 weight lines to assist the fly caster in delicate presentations. As the line weight increased, the taper was reduced in length to compensate for the heavier flies being cast. In 1993, the 444 series was improved again with the introduction of the 444 LAZER line series. LAZER lines have hard coatings and internal lubricants and long belly sections to aid in longer casts.

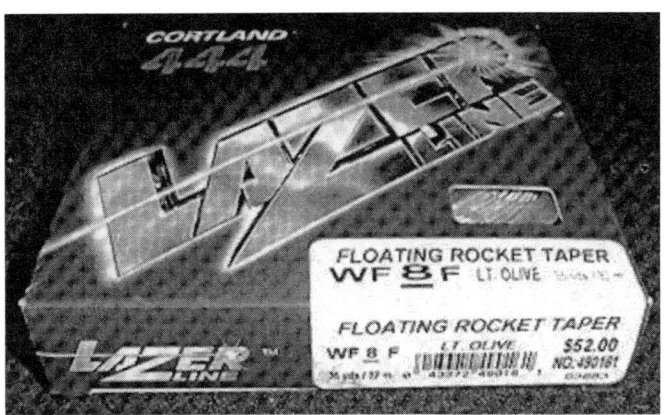

CORTLAND 444 LAZER LINE

Cortland also continued making acquisitions. In 1985 it purchased Precision Sports, Inc.—an importer of hunting, shooting and outdoor products. This was followed in 1988 when Cortland purchased Aqualine, a producer of braided fishing lines. It also purchased Rodon Manufacturing, Inc., a manufacturer of aluminum fishing rod cases and component parts for fly rod building. On October 1, 1999, Cortland acquired Masterline, a major

U.K. fly line manufacturer.

Recently, Cortland introduced the 555 line series. These lines feature a mono core that has lumens (triangular, horizontal hollow sections) inside the core to enhance floating. The 555 has a dual coating system consisting of a durable inner plastic coating and then a second outer coating that is very slick coupled with taper designs to promote long casts. The 555 comes in several different configurations including a clear floating line.

It is the rare fisherman who has not used and appreciated one or more of Cortland's fly lines. For over 85 years, Cortland has a tradition of making lines for all skill levels. This starts with the economical Fairplay series that has been produced for over 70 years for the beginning fly fisherman and goes through the 555, which is a highly advanced line series. Cortland also has a wide suite of specialty tapered lines that can be seen on its web site at www.cortlandline.com, or at one of the hundreds of Pro Shops that carry its lines. Cortland also continues its long tradition of making lines for other firms that do not produce their own fly lines.

CORTLAND 555 LINE

NEWTON LINE COMPANY

The Newton Line Company (Newton) was founded by D. D. Newton, M. A. Whiting and A. W. Gibbs in 1909 in Homer, New York on the banks of the Tioughnioga River. Its initial plant burned down in 1917 and a new one was built. Over time, D. D. Newton withdrew from the firm. Newton was then reorganized in 1933 under the leadership of Edward D. O'Connell and then his son, Bob O'Connell.[80][81]

Newton grew quickly from having 200 braiding machines in 1909 to 1,000 machines in 1928. Its fishing motto was "a line for every fish that swims."

Newton's early enameled line was the Huckleberry Finn series and its silk fly lines were the Big Strike, Gray Phantom and the Streamline series. Newton was marketing its Streamline series in 1936. It was very popular with its "Newtonized" finish that helped the line cast straight and prevent kinks. Additionally, Newton used an enameled finish on its Brook Trout fly line series.

NEWTON POSTER

NEWTON'S HUCKLEBERRY FINN ENAMELED LINE

During WWII, Newton made parachute cord, sutures, and shot cord. Its employees subscribed 100 percent for war savings stamps and bonds. In one 12-week period in 1942, they purchased enough bonds and stamps to buy a 75mm anti-aircraft gun for the war effort.

After WWII, Newton began to market its popular nylon Airline fly line series. The pre-WWII Gray Phantom series had also made the transition from silk to nylon construction. By 1954, Newton was marketing its nylon Ghost fly lines series selling for $10.00-$11.00 for tapered lines and for $1.85-$3.00 for level lines. Ghost lines were available in amber or foliage green colors.

NEWTON'S GHOST LINE

By 1955, Newton was using a PVC Plastisol finish on its Ghost fly lines, while continuing to sell its well-known Streamline silk and Airline nylon fly lines.

NEWTON'S AIRLINE NYLON LINE

Newton regularly field tested its products—sometimes with unexpected results. In late March and early April 1959, Newton employee Frank Carter and his party of seven other fishermen were fishing on Treasure Lake in central Cuba. On the second day, they returned to camp and found Fidel Castro and numerous of his bearded soldiers waiting for them. Castro had heard about their fishing trip and simply decided to join them. Since all the soldiers had guns, Frank Carter and his fellow fishermen eagerly welcomed Castro to their fishing trip. Castro stayed for seven days and then left.[82]

Castro has always been an active fisherman and won three trophy cups in 1960 at the Ernest Hemingway fishing tournament in Cuba. Clearly, the love of fishing and sports is a common denominator among men who may not agree on political issues.

FIDEL CASTRO AND ERNEST HEMINGWAY AT A 1960 FISHING TOURNAMENT
Courtesy of www.cubaphotogallery.com

Newton had a long history of making lines for uses other than fishing. As early as 1928, Newton was producing lines that went into cords for curtains, upholstery, radios and airplanes. In 1962, it formed a new company—Newton Filaments, Inc., to specialize in extruding polyethylene, polypropylene, and other new synthetic materials. Newton then decided in 1975 that its future lay in the industrial monofilament cordage and line business. It sold its Fishing Line Division to the Cortland Line Company in nearby Cortland, NY. Newton made significant contributions to the sport of fly fishing in its 66 years of existence and produced many fine fly lines.

MASTERLINE—U.K.

Anglers Masterline Limited (Masterline) was formed in the early 1970s by Philip Tallents and Terry Collingbourne. It is located in Tewkesbury, Gloucestershire, U.K., which is about 100 miles west of London where the Severn and Avon Rivers meet. Philip Tallents had previously been the managing director of Shakespeare Company, U.K. and Terry Collingbourne had been the technical manager at Shakespeare. Masterline started in a converted dairy and still remains at that location.[83]

Jack Martin was another key member of the of the early Masterline team. Martin was a four time world fly casting champion. He was also one of the founders of the Game Angling Instructors Association, an organization that teaches fly casting in the U.K. Jack Martin was able to articulate the needs of fly fishermen for

MASTERLINE LOGO
Courtesy of Cortland Line Company

Philip Tallents and Terry Collingbourne to put into their designs. The first Masterline fly lines had traditional PVC coatings.

Soon after forming Masterline, Philip Tallents became friends with Philip Dunn who was the technical director of British Insulated Callender Cables (BICC). BICC was the largest manufacturer of plastic insulated cable in the U.K. and had most of the technology needed to make extruded fly lines. Terry Collingbourne filed a U.S. patent application on June 22, 1972 for extruded fly lines with inert gas bubbles to aid in the lines' flotation. Patent number 3,830,009 was issued for this process on August 20, 1974. Masterline had BICC manufacture extruded lines for them using the joint Masterline-BICC technologies until the mid 1980s, when Masterline purchased its own extrusion machinery.

In addition to selling fly lines in the U.K., Masterline also began distributing lines in the U.S. through a relationship with Sunset Line and Twine, which ended in 1978. This was followed with a similar relationship with Gudebrod, which ended in the 1980s. Masterline also produced lines for a variety of U.S. companies including Orvis, Thomas and Thomas, McKenzie and Redington. Unfavorable exchange rates between U.S. and U.K. currencies ultimately led to Masterline deciding not to provide its lines to the U.S. market.

Masterline manufactured a large number of fly line series over the years including:

Advantage
Banker
Chalkstream—a very popular line in the U.S.
Challenge
Chancellor
Co-ed
Debut
Don
Graduate
Jubilee
Maxim
Oxbridge
Pioneer
Revolution
Shadow
Sportsman
Target
XL

In the early 1980s, Masterline allowed Ryobi Limited of Japan to buy into the firm

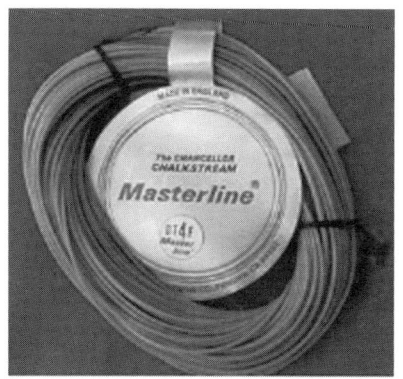

MASTERLINE CHALKSTREAM LINE

MASTERLINE SHADOW SERIES

and the firm's name was changed to Ryobi Masterline Limited. This partnership flourished for several years until Ryobi was impacted by the Japanese financial crisis of the mid 1990s. A Masterline management team led by Dick Tallents (Philip Tallents' son) bought the firm in 1998 and then sold it in October, 1999 to Cortland Line Company (Cortland).

Cortland recently decided to transfer all the Masterline manufacturing capabilities from the U.K. to Cortland, NY from which it will supply U.S. made Masterline fly lines to the U.K. and Europe. The Masterline brand will continue on given its long and proud history. Masterline also has an excellent web site at www.thenumberone.co.uk

BERKLEY

Berkley was started in 1937 when 16-year old Berkley Bedell took some of his newspaper delivery earnings and began selling flies to local tackle shops and vacationing anglers. He continued this business while in high school. After attending Iowa State and serving in the Army Air Corps, he returned in 1945 to Spirit Lake, Iowa to start Berkley Fly Company (Berkley).

BERKLEY BEDELL AS A TEENAGER TYING FLIES
Courtesy of Outdoor Technologies Group

One of Berkley's first products was cable wire leaders. Berkley developed a process for a nylon-coated wire leader that was called Steelon. This was followed in 1956 with Dew Flex monofilament fishing line. In 1959, ongoing research and development created the company's breakthrough innovation—Trilene line. Trilene became known throughout the world and its popularity propelled the company to rapid growth. This growth has been well-recognized. President Lyndon Johnson awarded Berkley Bedell the Small Businessman of the Year award in 1964.

BERKLEY STEELON ADVERTIZING SIGN

Berkley manufactured braided products for many years. It entered the fly line business when it purchased the Marathon Line Company (Marathon) in the 1960s. Marathon had developed a fly line series called the Golden Zephyr, which was a good line for its time. It had a foamed polyurethane extruded coating over a braided line core. Berkley introduced its own Golden Zephyr series in 1966.

BERKLEY PERMA FLOAT LINE

The Golden Zephyr series was followed by a Silver Glide series that used an extruded PVC coating instead of the extruded polyurethane coating associated with the Golden Zephyr lines. The taper in the Silver Glide series was developed by varying the speed of the line as it went through the extrusion machine. Fast speeds resulted in smaller diameter line portions and slower speeds resulted in larger diameter line portions. These lines were built for the mass retailing portion of the market.[84]

Berkley wanted to develop a "higher end" fly line and continued its fly line development. Extrusion of fly lines was ceased in 1972. Berkley's Danny Foote filed a patent application in late 1973 for a two layer PVC coated line. Patent 3,868,785 was issued for this invention on March 4, 1975. The inner coating was level and had large microballoons and as such, provided most of the line's flotation. The outer coating was tapered and had smaller microballoons giving it a hard finish. This patent also described an iris diaphragm system for applying the tapered coatings.

United States Patent [19]
Foote

[11] **3,868,785**
[45] **Mar. 4, 1975**

[54] **FLYLINE FOR FISHING**

[75] Inventor: **Danny R. Foote**, Spirit Lake, Iowa

[73] Assignee: **Berkley & Company, Inc.**, Spirit Lake, Iowa

[22] Filed: **Dec. 7, 1973**

[21] Appl. No.: **422,715**

[52] U.S. Cl. **43/44.98**
[51] Int. Cl. **A01k 91/00**
[58] Field of Search .... 43/44.98; 117/161, 161 P; 161/175

[56] **References Cited**
UNITED STATES PATENTS

2,862,282	12/1958	Beebe	43/44.98
3,043,045	7/1962	Martuch	43/44.98
3,334,436	8/1967	Cole, Jr.	43/44.98
3,486,266	12/1969	Richardson et al.	43/44.98
3,512,294	5/1970	Howald	43/44.98
3,523,034	8/1970	Howald	43/44.98

Primary Examiner—Warner H. Camp

[57] **ABSTRACT**

A flyline for fishing which comprises a core with a plurality of individual coatings, each containing microballoons and in certain instances, other fillers being applied thereover. The core comprises a generally continuous filament extending axially along the length of the line. A first coating is arranged over the core, with the first coating comprising a plastic matrix retaining a certain quantity of microballoons therein. The second coating is arranged over the first coating and comprises a plastic matrix retaining a different quantity of microballoons, with the microballoons in the second coating being smaller in diameter, and being included in a lesser percentage than in the first coating so as to provide a composite line with significant buoyancy determined primarily by the inner coating and with a finish determined by a harder and more dense outer shell. While the first or inner coating is normally of constant wall thickness, the second or outer coating may be tapered so as to provide a tapered diameter line.

14 Claims, 3 Drawing Figures

BERKLEY'S DANNY FOOTE PATENT

In 1975, Berkley introduced its Specialist line series, based on its newly patented dual coating technology which provided excellent flotation characteristics. This was important as market research had repeatedly shown that one of the biggest problems with floating lines during that period was that their tip sections sank. The Specialist line series was targeted for the specialty fly shop market, but ended up being an "upper end" line in the mass retailing market. After a few years, the Specialist line series was redesigned to a one coating construction. The New Dimension line series was also introduced in this time period. It was an inexpensive single coated line, again aimed at the mass retailing marketplace.

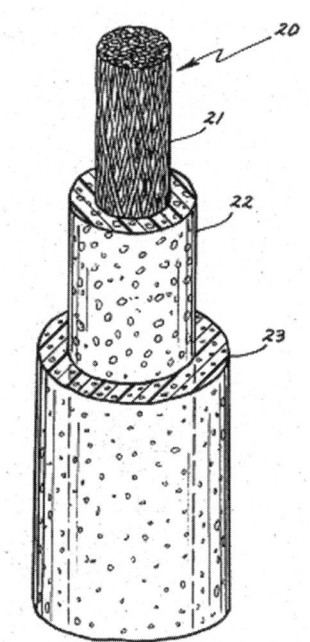

DRAWING FROM BERKLEY'S DANNY FOOTE PATENT

BERKLEY SPECIALIST FLY LINE

In 1979, Berkley Bedell's son, Tom, took over leadership of the firm and since that time has guided its extensive growth. In 1988, Berkley purchased Fenwick and a new organization called Outdoors Technologies Group (OTG) was formed to allow bringing together companies like Berkley and Fenwick under one umbrella. In 1995, OTG purchased Abu Garcia, giving it four of the best-known fishing equipment brands in the history of the sport.

The 1990s saw a number of additional changes in OTG's fly line business. OTG decided to begin switching all of its fly line manufacturing to the Fenwick label. In the transition period, the Berkley Advanta series of lines was introduced using the Specialist's line series tapers and the new flotation construction techniques developed for the new Fenwick lines. The Naturalist line series was also developed. 1996 saw the termination of the venerable Specialist series, which had been Berkley's best known fly line for over two decades.

BERKLEY ADVANTA LINE

Today with Trilene, Fenwick, Abu Garcia, Power Bait, and dozens of other fishing and outdoor products, Berkley is one of the major forces in the world-wide sport fishing industry. Of note is that Berkley's parent company name has recently been changed from Outdoors Technologies Group to Pure Fishing. Berkley has also established a museum in Spirit Lake, Iowa that is open to the public. It has a fine collection of the firm's historic fishing products and equipment. Berkley also has an excellent web sites at www.berkley-fishing.com and www.purefishing.com.

MARATHON

The Marathon Line Company (Marathon) was formed in circa 1937 in Marathon, New York (NY) by Jim Frye and Carl Hubbard. Jim Frye was knowledgeable about the fishing line business as his father-in law was a past president of Newton Line Company. After a short period of time, Marathon moved to Homer, NY and Charles Briggs bought out the interest of Carl Hubbard. Briggs was active in managing the sales side of the business with his two sons-in-law, Ted Harris and Mike Norris. Marathon's marketing theme of "best in the long run" tied back to the firm's name and its lines had the distinctive symbol of a marathon runner on them.[85]

Marathon was initially known for its Supreme series of silk lines.

MARATHON SUPREME FLY LINE

Marathon was active in war production during WWII—making parachute cord, shot cord, sutures, and so forth. The plant worked 24 hours per day, every day, including holidays.

When nylon came into common use, Marathon developed its Perma Float nylon series of lines. This line came in a transparent polystyrene utility box.

MARATHON PERMA FLOAT LINE

In the 1960s Marathon developed a line series called Golden Zephyr which had a foamed polyurethane coating over a braided line. Berkley then bought Marathon in order to enter the fly line manufacturing business. Berkley's Perma Float line series and 1966 Golden Zephyr line series were the successors to Marathon's Perma Float and Golden Zephyr series.[86]

Marathon was never a large company in terms of the quantity of lines produced. It did produce excellent fly lines. It also will be remembered as the firm that Berkley bought and used to provide Berkley's aggressive entrance into the fly line manufacturing business.

FENWICK

Fenwick was formed in 1954/55 by six local Seattle area businessmen who started making fiberglass rods in a garage near Lake Fenwick, Washington—thus the firm's name. The original Fenwick owners then sold the firm to the Sevenstrand Tackle Company (Sevenstrand). Sevenstrand was then purchased by the family of Philip T. Clock. By 1978, Philip Clock was having health problems and Fenwick was sold to Woodstream Corporation. In approximately 1988, Woodstream was purchased by Ekco and soon after the Fenwick portion of Woodstream was sold to Outdoors Technologies Group (Berkley).

Fenwick has been a great rod maker throughout its history. It is the rare fly fisherman who has not owned or used a Fenwick fly rod somewhere along the way. Fenwick also began to sell fly lines in late 1969 and sold them through 1974.[87] These lines were made to its specifications by Scientific Anglers and were called Master Class lines. They came in level, double tapered and weight forward configurations.

Fenwick was arguably the first firm to make graphite fly rods, starting in 1974. It concentrated on the new graphite fly rod and discontinued its line sales. This remained the case even after it joined Berkley (Outdoor Technologies Group) in 1988.

In April 1991, Berkley decided to revitalize the Fenwick brand name for manufacturing fly lines and started making Fenwick lines at Berkley's Spirit Lake, Iowa plant. Several veteran Fenwick fly fishing equipment experts including Vic Cutter and Dale Barnes helped in the fly line designs. The first series of fly lines were called World Class and had several subset line groups: Trout Class, Bass Class, Steelhead Class and Sea Class lines. The reason for the subset groups of lines was that Fenwick felt a single taper design was not fully appropriate for all types of fishing.

FENWICK WORLD CLASS II LINE

A succession of new Fenwick fly lines soon followed.

1994—Profile lines introduced. These were economical lines that were subsequently introduced in Canada in 2000.

FENWICK MASTER CLASS LINE

FENWICK PROFILE LINE

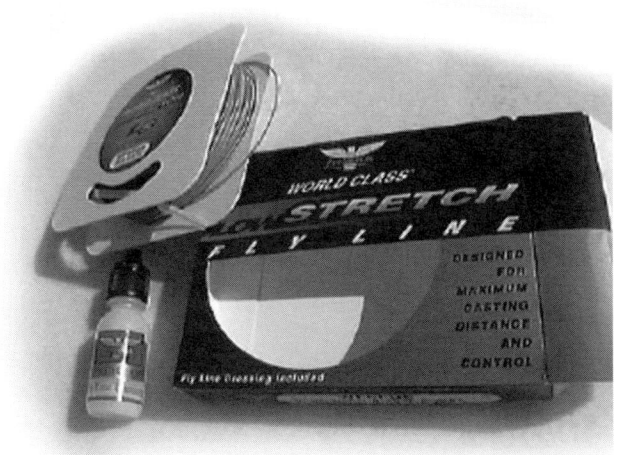

FENWICK WORLD CLASS LOW STRETCH LINE

1996—World Class II Trout, Bass, Salmon and Sea Class series introduced.

1996—World Class Low Stretch line series introduced. These lines had one strand of Kevlar in the core to cut down on stretching.

2001—World Class SF introduced.

Fenwick is a well-respected brand of lines world-wide. We can expect Berkley to continue to develop new line series under the Fenwick name.

ABU

Abu was founded in 1921 by Carl Borgstrom in Svangsta, Sweden. Abu was originally in the pocket watch and taximeter manufacturing business. WWII created the situation in Sweden where there was no export of its taximeters. WWII had also stopped the importing of fishing equipment into Sweden and consequently, there was significant demand for reels and rods. Abu decided to make reels, which ultimately resulted in the famous Ambassador reel.

Following WWII, Abu began exporting the firm's products outside Scandinavia. In 1954, Garcia got the U.S. distribution rights to the Abu Ambassador reel. Previously, Garcia had obtained the rights for Mitchell reels from France.

Historically, Abu had a relatively small presence in the U.S. and European fly fishing equipment markets. Abu had fly lines made to its specifications primarily by Scientific Anglers in the U.S. and Masterline in the U.K.[88]

ABU LINE (C. 1964)

In 1976, a majority interest in Abu was sold to the Swedish Incentive Group. The Incentive Group through Abu then bought Garcia in 1978. By the time of the Garcia acquisition, it was decided to de-emphasize fly fishing equipment and concentrate on the Ambassador and Garcia reels. As such, fly fishing equipment, including lines, was only a very small part of its overall business. In 1995, Outdoor Technologies Group purchased Abu Garcia.

GARCIA

The Garcia Company was an importer in the 1920s and 1930s. One of the things it imported was silkworm "gut" from China, which was used by doctors in sutures. The Garcia Company then got the idea to also use this material as leader material for fly rods and went into that business. In the mid-1940s, the Garcia Company also got the U.S. distributorship for the French "Mitchell" spinning reel. In about 1960, Garcia also bought Conolon and became one of the major fiberglass rod makers in the U.S.

In the same time era, Garcia gained control of the Horton Manufacturing Company (Horton) line manufacturing operations located in Rockville, Connecticut (CT). Garcia then used Horton's famous "Kingfisher" name on some of the Garcia lines. It also developed a Dick Wolff Autograph fly line (circa 1964). Dick Wolff was a Garcia executive and a well-known writer who had written a book on fishing tackle and techniques.[89] This was followed in the early 1970s with a series of nylon fly lines endorsed by Lee Wulff.

GARCIA FLY LINE

GARCIA LEE WULFF LINE

GARCIA KINGFISHER LINE

In 1978, Abu bought the fishing part of Garcia, which was in bankruptcy. Garcia's line-making operations faded away and in 1995 Abu Garcia became part of Outdoors Technologies Group (Berkley).

HORTON MANUFACTURING COMPANY (BRISTOL AND KINGFISHER BRANDS)

Everett Horton was born in Bristol, Connecticut (CT) in 1836 and was a very energetic and mechanically-oriented person. He went to California in 1858 via the Isthmus of Panama for the Gold Rush, and afterwards came back to Connecticut and started several manufacturing businesses. In 1886, after developing and patenting a steel-telescoping rod, Horton sold his patents to Charles Treadway, Frank Hayward and Charles Pope. In 1888, these three men started the Horton Manufacturing Company (HMC) in Bristol, CT to make steel rods under the Bristol brand.[90] [91]

HMC grew by internal growth and acquisition. In 1916, it bought out B. F. Meek & Sons of Frankfort, Kentucky (KY) which made the famous Meek and Blue Grass Reels. The Meek brothers had made these reels since 1835. All of the reel making equipment and many of the Meek reel makers were moved to HMC's operation in Bristol, CT.

HORTON MANUFACTURING CO. 1925 AD

In 1919, HMC acquired the line-making business of Elisha J. Martin in Rockville, CT. Martin was one of the first U.S. manufacturers to use braided silk in fishing lines. His brand was called Kingfisher. When Elisha Martin died in 1898, his son (A. Leroy Martin) took over the business until it was acquired by HMC. After HMC's acquisition, the line-making operations stayed in Rockville, CT. Kingfisher lines were treated by a number of different methods (waterproofing, enameling, and so forth) depending on their intended usage.

EARLY BRISTOL CATALOG

These early HMC lines had the following characteristics:

- **Variegated** —A moderate price line that had been waterproofed.
- **Russet Enamel**—A medium-weight enameled line suitable for fly fishing as well as other forms of fishing.
- **Kingfisher Oiled Silk**—This was the Bristol brand "flagship" line. It was made of raw silk with the gum of the silkworm left in to add to the line's toughness. These lines were then saturated and coated with water-

excluding oils. Finally, they were coated with a thin coat of enamel.
- **Extra Quality Trout Line**—Small diameter lines for light trout fishing. They were made in one diameter of 10 pound test with three different finishes (STO-Oil Finish, STE-Enameled Finish and STR-Russet Enameled Finish).
- **Potomac Bass**—A strong line for bass fishing (16 pound test) again made in three finishes (PBO-Oiled, PBE-Enameled and PBR-Russet Enameled Finish).

HMC's strategy of manufacturing Bristol rods, Meek reels and Kingfisher lines allowed it to market all three as a package.

In 1940, a Kingfisher De Luxe double tapered fly line sold for $6.50 for 30-yards. In 1941, HMC also was marketing its Kingfisher Luckie series. Additionally in 1942, it was marketing its Kingfisher Perma Flex series.

HORTON KINGFISHER DE LUXE LINE

HMC did not just manufacture fishing equipment. In 1921, it was one of the first, if not the first, firms to make steel shafts for golf clubs. It also sold golf balls, bags and accessories. In 1951, HMC was sold to an investment group from New York and Cincinnati. It was subsequently merged into the Wright Machine Company of Worchester, MA where it was known as the Bristol Horton Division.

Garcia subsequently took control of the Rockville line operations and it used the famous "Kingfisher" name on some of its lines. In 1978, Abu bought the fishing part of Garcia (which was in bankruptcy) and then in 1995 Abu Garcia became part of Outdoors Technologies Group (Berkley).

KINGFISHER POSTER (c. 1911)

> **Chain stores and catalog stores**
>
> **Montgomery Ward (1872), Sears (1893) and Western Auto (1909)**
> **Abercrombie & Fitch (1892)**
> **Herter's (1893)**

MONTGOMERY WARD, SEARS AND WESTERN AUTO

Given the phenomenal advances in general transportation and current easy access to quality goods and services, it is sometimes hard to remember how important chain stores and catalog sales firms were to the average citizen in the first half of the Twentieth Century. Montgomery Ward started as a mail order business in 1872 and was followed by Sears, Roebuck and Company (Sears) starting in 1893. Western Auto Supply Company (Western) was founded in 1909. By 1954, Sears had 694 retail stores and annually mailed out 50 million catalogs. At one point it was estimated that of every $100 spent for general merchandise in the United States, $5 went to Sears.

Since the fishing public wanted fly lines, Sears and its fellow catalog and chain store competitors had them made to their specifications by others and then resold them. There was a line for every budget. J. C. Higgins fishing tackle, which was sold by Sears, had an enameled cotton fly line for the low budget fisherman. Western Auto similarly had its Good Luck enameled line.

For the higher-end fishing line users, Sears had its Xpert silk line series. Montgomery Ward had its competitive Sport King and Amber King silk line series. Western Auto similarly had its Revelation silk line series.

SEARS XPERT LINE

J.C. HIGGINS FLOATING NYLON LINE

MONTGOMERY WARD AMBER KING LINE

Following WWII, thousands of fishermen wanted ready access to the new generation of nylon and better-floating lines. America's retailers (both mail order firms and chain store outlets) met this demand by first purchasing and then reselling large numbers of these new nylon lines. This business arrangement, in turn, allowed the line manufacturing industry to flourish and continue the development of the modern fly line. Our family, and millions of others like us, got its first fly lines from a "chain store" retailer near our home.

In 1952, Western Auto was still marketing its popular Revelation series that was then available in nylon.

TED WILLIAMS

WESTERN AUTO REVELATION SILK LINE

Sears was also actively marketing fly lines. Ted Williams (the Hall of Fame baseball player and active fisherman) helped Sears develop a very successful series of fly lines.

SEARS TED WILLIAMS LINE

The historic contribution of the mail order and chain store retailers to fly fishing has been great and has often been forgotten in this age of specialty fly fishing stores.

ABERCROMBIE & FITCH

Abercrombie & Fitch was founded in 1892 by David T. Abercrombie and Ezra M. Fitch. Abercrombie was a former prospector, miner, inventor and railway engineer who was making camping gear in New York City. Ezra Fitch was a successful but bored lawyer and a member of the sporting-gentlemen elite. It was a partnership of opposites with the rough edged Abercrombie and the gentleman, Fitch. Arguments ensued over the direction the firm should take and Abercrombie left the business in 1907 to again make camping equipment. Fitch developed the business to serve the "rich and famous" and had great success. By the time Fitch retired in 1928, Abercrombie & Fitch's New York City store on Madison Avenue store was generally known as "The Greatest Sporting Goods Store in the World."[92]

Subsequent presidents of Abercrombie & Fitch were also members of the "gentry" and the store continued its upscale image. It was the New York City store where Teddy Roosevelt went to get outfitted for his upcoming campaign in Cuba. Admiral Richard Byrd outfitted several of his polar trips at the store, and Charles Lindbergh was outfitted there for his trip across the Atlantic. The store also made service and salesman knowledge of its products top priorities. Catalogs were sent out each year to 350,000 people and the catalogs stated the New York City store was "Where the Blazed Trail Crosses the Boulevard."[93]

Fly fishing was important to Abercrombie and Fitch. A casting pool was built on the roof of the Madison Avenue store where serious fly fishermen could test out the store's fly fishing equipment. Leo Martin, the store's tackle buyer, authored a 1957 book on fly tying.

Abercrombie & Fitch historically sold a wide range of fly lines it had made to its specifications by other firms, such as Gladding. One of its popular lines was the Monogram

INTERIOR OF AN ABERCROMBIE & FITCH STORE (1938)

Banty series, which matched its popular Banty fly rod.

ABERCROMBIE & FITCH BANTY LINE

By 1958, the firm had opened stores in Hyannis, Massachusetts; Chicago and San Francisco. Continued expansion to four other "high-end" locations did not work economically and by 1977 the company went bankrupt. A year or so after the bankruptcy, Oshmans bought the Abercrombie & Fitch name and tried to revive the operation by opening a new store in Beverly Hills, California in 1979. Oshmans then sold the Abercrombie & Fitch name to The Limited—a retail chain clothing store. In 1996, Abercrombie and Fitch went on the New York Stock Exchange and in 1998, it was spun off from The Limited. Today, most young people think of Abercrombie and Fitch solely as a firm that sells modern clothing.

Abercrombie & Fitch was a unique firm that provided excellent fly fishing equipment to those who could afford it and dreams of owning the same equipment to those could not afford it. Its fly fishing tradition is missed.

HERTER'S

Herter's retailing tradition can be traced back to 1893. Edward O. Herter was born in 1876 in Fairbault, Minnesota and at the age of approximately eighteen, moved to Waseca, Minnesota. He soon went into the retail clothing and dry goods business in a store named Beehive. In 1901, Edward Herter married and had two children—a daughter, Margaret, and a son, George Leonard Herter (born in 1922).

George Herter graduated from high school in Waseca and then attended the University of Minnesota. George followed his father's retailing career by starting what we know as Herter's in his Waseca, Minnesota garage. George Herter initially sold feathers to fly fishermen, followed by duck decoys and other outdoor sports equipment. Then, similar to millions of other Americans, George's career was interrupted by WWII during which he served four years in the Army. He quickly resumed his business after the war and issued Herter's first post-WWII catalog in 1946.[94]

Herter's complete line of sporting goods, which matched its motto of "Tenacious For Quality," soon captured a significant portion of the nation's post-WWII urge to enjoy the outdoors. The firm prospered and at its peak operations, mailed out approximately 500,000 catalogs per year—each having more than 500 pages. The resulting business required Herter's to fill 3,000-4,000 orders daily out of a product line of 20,000 items utilizing a staff of 300. It had six stores located in Waseca and Glenwood, Minnesota; Olympia, Washington; Mitchell, South Dakota; Iowa Falls, Iowa and Beaver Dam, Wisconsin.

Herter's fly lines were made to its specifications by others. Its Masterweave fly line series was very popular by the 1950s. Herter's 1955 catalog featured the Masterweave fly line. It was made of woven Tynex nylon and covered with a sheath of solid Tynex nylon. In typical Herter's marketing bravado, it advertised this line as "unconditionally guaranteed to last years longer than any fly line made in the world." Masterweave tapered lines sold for $4.85 in 1955. Also featured in its 1955 catalog was the 14 foot tapered spinning fly line, which sold for $3.95. It was designed for use with spinning rods.

HERTER'S SUPREME SINKING LINE

Two of Herter's other popular fly lines were the Cuxhaven and Supreme line series.

HERTER'S SUPREME FLOATING LINE

HERTER'S 1955 CATALOG

In the period between 1955 and Herter's 1972-73 catalog, the cost of Masterweave lines had actually decreased. Masterweave Floating and Sinking lines now sold for $2.75 for tapered lines. Its higher end Imperial floating lines were advertised as needing "absolutely no line dressing to make them float". These lines sold for $1.77 for level lines and $3.83 for tapered lines.

In 1972, Herter's catalog operations were moved to Mitchell, South Dakota and the firm began to experience financial problems due to over expansion. In 1977, the business was sold to Marshall Seeburg Sons of Chicago, Illinois who filed for bankruptcy in 1981. George Herter died in 1994 and will long be remembered for his many contributions in helping people enjoy hunting, fishing and many other outdoor activities.

The Herter's operation remained dormant for several years and a new organization reintroduced a smaller version of the Herter's catalog in 1990. Today, Herter's is part of Overtons, Inc., which is located in Greenville, South Carolina. Overtons' uses the Herter's name on a series of waterfowl hunting supplies. Cabela's provides the distribution of these Herter's products—see www.herters.com

Chapter Three
FLY LINES POST-WWII
Pent-up demand

The fishing line and tackle business changed dramatically after WWII. People had extra money to spend and there was a pent-up demand for fishing equipment. Gadabout Gaddis (a colorful TV fishing celebrity and tackle salesman) said it this way, *Probably the best way I can describe this frantic demand is by comparing the volumes of sales in my seven-state territory. When I took it over in 1929, it was producing $20,000 in total business. By 1948 I was selling between $800,000 and $1,000,000 a year even though I had given up half of New York State by then. I mean to tell you, mister, the tackle industry was skyrocketing.*[95]

The number of sport fishermen wanting new equipment was huge. In 1948, 14,582,739 people bought freshwater fishing licenses and an estimated additional 8,000,000 people fished in saltwater, where licenses were not required.[96] The post-WWII invention of the fiberglass rod plus the new spinning reel also helped precipitate this new demand. The public could now get durable fiberglass rods and easy-to-cast spinning reels at reasonable prices.

Fly line technology had made slow but steady progress from its horsehair days through its silk pre-WWII era. Unfortunately, the inherent problems with silk lines were not totally solved by WWII. They were still prone to rot and had to be routinely "dressed" and dried to maintain their flotation.

GADABOUT GADDIS

New materials appear and are adopted into fly line construction

Nylon

Nature provided us with many excellent fibers (silk, cotton, linen, and so forth). It took chemists a long time to make synthetic fibers that were as good as the natural ones. The first significant synthetic fiber developed was rayon in 1910. This fiber started with cotton or tree pulp cellulose that, in turn, was made into a synthetic fiber. Acetate followed in 1924 and, along with rayon, became the dominant new synthetic fibers until the much less expensive wonder fiber, nylon, was invented.

Nylon was not an overnight invention. The search for it began in 1926 at DuPont with the formation of a new department to do fundamental research into chemistry. Fundamental research had the object of discovering new scientific facts. This was a change from DuPont's previous policy towards research, which was applied research. In applied research, previously established scientific facts were used to solve practical problems.

Wallace Hume Carothers, a brilliant chemist, was hired in 1928 to lead the new fundamental research effort at DuPont. Carothers was a well-rounded person with many non-chemistry interests including fishing. Unfortunately, he suffered from depression. This clinical condition was to haunt him all his life.[97]

Carothers and his research team worked at finding new chemistry facts. The result of all their work was that nylon was invented in 1934 in a DuPont laboratory. This new fiber was called Nylon 66 and was the first fiber made entirely from chemical ingredients through a chemical process called polymerization. This laboratory nylon fiber was stronger and more abrasion-resistant than silk, which made it a potentially significant new fiber. In 1937, enough additional research had been completed for DuPont to file patents for nylon. Three weeks after the patents were filed, Carothers took his own life during a period of major depression. His death was a tragic loss, but life had to continue and DuPont continued on.

WALLACE CAROTHERS
Courtesy of the Hagley Museum and Library

WALLACE CAROTHERS (LEFT) WITH FRIEND (CIRCA 1935)
Courtesy of the Chemical Heritage Foundation

DuPont decided to aim its new nylon fiber at the women's silk hosiery market. Each woman in America needed an average of eight pairs per year so there was a ready market. Nylon was announced on October 27, 1938 at a meeting of three thousand women. They were gathered at the site for the 1939 New York World's Fair. Nylon hose went on sale in May, 1940 and women immediately loved the new fiber.

*WOMEN'S NYLON HOSE—
GIANT LEG ADVERTISEMENT
Courtesy of the Hagley Museum and Library*

Nylon did not rot and lose its strength like natural fibers such as silk or linen. It could also be finely extruded into unlimited lengths. On January 20, 1939, Ashaway started marketing Ashaway Nylon Bait Casting Line, which was the first commercial product made of nylon.[98] Women's hose, the DuPont target product, did not appear in stores for another 18 months.

Prior to WWII, the new nylon lines were not overly popular with fishermen because the inherent properties of nylon made it stretch easily. Stretching was good for nylon stockings, but the same stretch quality made it hard to hook a fish on a long line. When nylon was used in fly line cores, the braided nylon threads also stretched easily, and the surface flotation finish did not. This condition was further complicated by the fact that nylon threads are virtually non-absorptive and the finishing oils used at that time did not work into them, as they did into silk. Braid and finish often parted due to these factors.[99]

Additionally, nylon was a significantly lighter material than silk. Thus, nylon lines needed to be bigger in diameter to impart the same loading on a rod, as contrasted to their silk counterparts. The bulkier nylon lines also did not cast as well in windy conditions and nylon still had flotation issues. The flotation issues were due to a variety of reasons. One major reason was that nylon (having a specific gravity of roughly 1.2) is heavier than water.[100] Anything over 1.0 in specific gravity naturally tends to sink as soon as the water's surface tension effect is overcome.

WWII mandated other uses for nylon. It was used for parachutes, airplane tire reinforcement, glider tow ropes, and so forth. Following WWII, DuPont continued its research into synthetic fibers and numerous new synthetic fibers were invented. Of interest to fishermen was that Dacron (i.e., polyester fiber) was invented in the early 1950s and Kevlar was invented in 1965. Of all the new synthetic fibers in the Twentieth Century, nylon was arguably the most important.

Post-WWII, the stretch in nylon filaments was reduced through the use of new technology. Nylon gradually became the fly line of choice, as it did not require the care and attention that silk and linen lines required. Since nylon was inherently lighter than silk, it required the fly line buyer to have some knowledge of the two line materials (silk versus nylon) in order to get the right line for their fly rod.

A.J. McClane in the July 1952 *Field & Stream* magazine wrote an article called "Fit the line to the rod" that described his view of the correct nylon and silk fly type fly lines for bamboo and fiberglass rods.

ROD	LEVEL LINE		DOUBLE TAPER		THREE TAPER	
	NYLON	*SILK*	*NYLON*	*SILK*	*NYLON*	*SILK*
BAMBOO						
7 1/2 to 8 feet 3 1/2 to 4 1/2 ounces	E	F	HDH	HEH	HDG	HEG
8 1/2 to 9 feet 4 1/2 to 5 1/4 ounces	D	E	HCH	HDH	HCF	HDG
9 feet 5 1/2 to 6 1/2 ounces	C	D	GBG	HCH	GBF	HCF
9 to 9 1/2 feet 6 1/2 to 7 1/2 ounces	B	C	FAF	GBG	GAF	GBF
GLASS						
7 1/2 to 8 feet 4 to 5 ounces	D	E	HCH	HDH	GBF	HCG
8 1/2 to 9 feet 5 1/4 to 6 ounces	C	D	HCH	HCH	GAF	GBF
9 feet 6 to 7 ounces	B	C	GBG	GBG	GAF	GAF
9 to 9 1/2 feet 7 to 8 1/2 ounces	B	B	FAF	GBG	G2AF	G2AF

Note: Three taper are torpedo-tapered or weight forward lines

Plastic line coatings

Fly fishermen in the early 1940s still did not like the fact that both the new nylon fly lines and their traditional silk fly lines did not float well without their ongoing maintenance and dressing. Line manufacturers responded to this concern by making new lines with new finishes.

Just before WWII, some of the first plastic-covered lines were made. American Line Company (which was under the control of Horrocks Ibbotson's management) developed a plastic fly line called Flex that was being sold in 1942.

Plastic was an obvious choice as a replacement for oiled finishes. The name "plastic" is given to plastics because they are pliable and can be easily shaped and molded. Just because they can be easily shaped and molded does not mean all plastics are soft forever. Some plastics end up being hard (e.g., keys on a computer) while others end up staying soft.

The key plastic compound used on fly lines is Polyvinyl Chloride, which is commonly called "PVC" or "vinyl." PVC is one of the most common synthetic materials used in the world. It was originally invented in a laboratory in Germany in 1872, but no commercial use was found for it. The German patents for PVC expired in 1925. In 1926, Waldo Semon (working for B. F. Goodrich) in essence reinvented PVC. Semon had the idea to use the waterproof material for shower curtains. Soon countless other uses were found for PVC. Semon was issued Patents 1,929,453 (1933) and 2,188,396 (1940) for his work.

Patented Oct. 10, 1933   1,929,453

UNITED STATES PATENT OFFICE

1,929,453

SYNTHETIC RUBBER-LIKE COMPOSITION
AND METHOD OF MAKING SAME

Waldo L. Semon, Silver Lake Village, Ohio, assignor to The B. F. Goodrich Company, New York, N. Y., a corporation of New York

No Drawing. Continuation of application Serial No. 320,003, November 16, 1928. This application September 17, 1932. Serial No. 633,686

18 Claims. (Cl. 260—6)

SEMON PATENT

When America's line manufacturers began developing plastic coatings, PVC was the material they used for almost all their line coatings. Of interest is that the vast majority of all line manufacturers today are still using PVC for line coatings. This is because PVC has the ability to be formulated in virtually an infinite number of ways. In the formulation process, chemical compounds are normally added to PVC to customize it for an intended use. For example, plasticizers are added to PVC coating which is used for coating fly lines to give them their needed flexibility. Pigments can be added to PVC to give lines different colors. For sinking lines, powdered heavy metals and/or solid glass balls are added to the PVC.

For the vast majority of fly lines in America, line coating technology since WWII can be thought of as an ongoing refinement of the basic PVC coating process to overcome problems associated with it

The manufacturers of the first generation of plastic-coated lines had numerous technical challenges to overcome. For example, just like the first post-WWII plastic seat covers on cars, the plasticizers in the PVC line coatings tended to leach out over time. The plastic PVC coating would then become brittle. With a line naturally bending due to casting, a brittle coating soon cracked. Manufacturers initially tried to overcome this problem by developing line cleaners that also had plasticizers in them. When fishermen cleaned their lines, they were also replacing some of the lost plasticizers. If fishermen did not clean their lines, then the lines became brittle much quicker.

A second challenge was that the fly line's nylon core did not easily bond to the PVC coating. Various primers were used on the nylon core to improve the bonding with the PVC coating.

A third challenge was that the new plastic coatings were heavier than water. When PVC and plasticizers are mixed together, the resulting mixture is called an "organosol" or more commonly it is called a "plastisol." The specific gravity of plastisols used for line coatings is often in the range of 1.3. Research has shown that fly lines having a specific gravity greater than 1.15 will not float.[101] In theory, anything with a specific gravity greater than 1.0 (the specific gravity of water) should sink, but the water's surface tension allows for floating of lines up to a specific gravity of 1.15. The nylon core in the line was also heavier than water, which further complicated the situation. Obviously, something else had to be added to the line to allow it to float.

The line manufacturing industry tried to address the flotation problem in a number of ways. They began to use different braiding techniques to get more void space in a line's core, which could then be used to hold air after the PVC coating was applied. Additionally, they began to create air bubbles in the coating to help the lines float. These air bubbles were created from steam generated from the natural moisture in the air and also from moisture in the line's core. The curing of the PVC coating required high temperatures, which enabled the generation of the steam. Air bubbles were a definite improvement in helping lines float.

The manufacturers of fly lines had to try and balance all these factors in their designs. They did not want to put a thick coating of PVC on the line. Its additional weight would tend to overcome the increased buoyancy that was generated by the air bubbles and air trapped inside the line. On the other hand, if the coating was too thin or if the plasticizers leached out, the line would crack. Water, once inside cracked lines, was difficult (if not impossible) to get out.

By the early 1950s, Cortland perfected its line manufacturing technology by braiding the tapered cores of its fly lines with a void in the center. When a level PVC coating was put on a tapered braided line, there was enough air entrapped inside the coating to make the line float. Cortland's 333 fly line, which came out in 1953, is generally considered the first successful floating plastic line. The 333 was an instant success.

CORTLAND 333 AD FROM 1955

The other line manufacturers were also similarly active. Soon, Gladding had its 1953 Aerofloat floating line that also had gas bubbles sealed into the line. These first generation PVC-coated lines were definite improvements over the previous oil finished silk and nylon lines. Unfortunately, these lines did not solve all the technical issues associated with plastic coated lines and additional research and technology was needed.

New manufacturing processes and materials appear

In the first generation of plastic line coatings, it was a challenge to get a uniform PVC coating on a tapered line core given all the problems associated with the early plastic coatings (plasticizer issues, core-coating bonding issues, air and gas flotation issues, and so forth).

Additionally, braided and tapered line cores still had to be made in the same historically slow labor-intensive way. To get a tapered line, the braiding machine operator had to periodically stop the braiding machine and either cut or insert a line to decrease or increase the line size. No two lines were ever exactly the same due to this laborious process. Braiding the cores with more void space to hold air created additional challenges.

The cost of tapered lines had to reflect all this effort and they were expensive. For example, a 1947 Gudebrod GudeKing silk line cost $11.00. That $11.00 cost in 1947 was the equivalent to $96 in 2001. In contrast, level braided lines could be easily and inexpensively made by machine in long continuous lengths. A 1948 Ashaway size H level nylon line cost $1.75 which would be the equivalent to $13.35 in 2001.[102] In 2001 dollars, it meant that the late 1940s line buyer had to pay the equivalent of about $80 more to get a tapered line as contrasted to a level line.

The next level of sophistication that was needed was figuring out how to put a variable-thickness plastic coating on a level line which would create a tapered fly line as a result of the process. If this could be done, it would create significant cost savings in fly line manufacturing, as the traditional expensive way of creating tapered cores could be eliminated.

At this point, Leon P. Martuch entered. In behalf of his firm, Scientific Anglers (SA), Martuch filed a patent application on January 13, 1954 for a "variable strand coating device."

This was a process in which a variable thickness of plastic coating could be applied to a level line. Patent 2,960,062 was issued for this process on November 15, 1960.

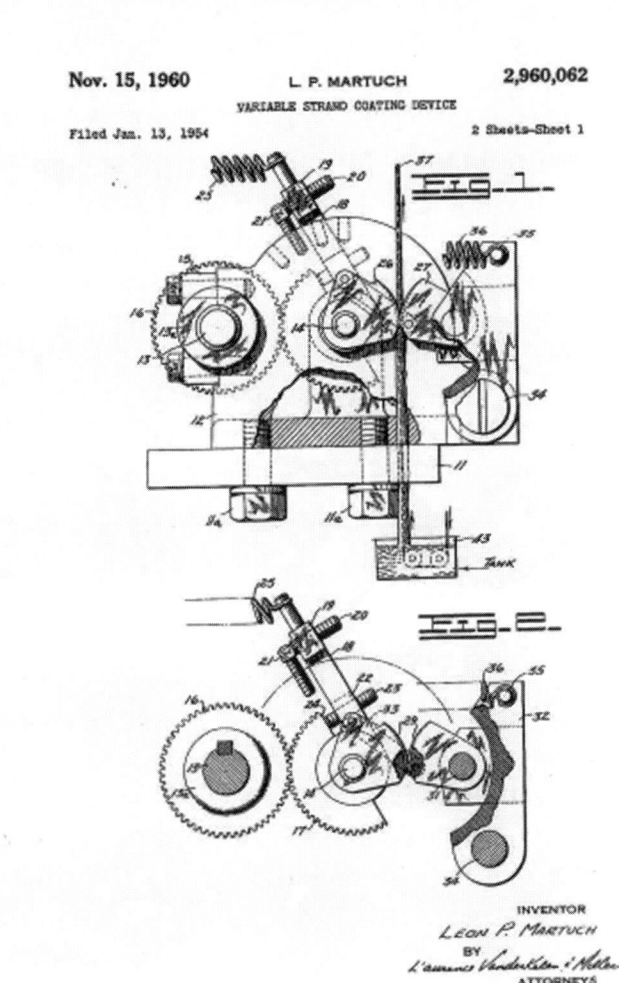

*FIRST MARTUCH PATENT—
FILED JANUARY 13, 1954*

Martuch's new coating equipment was a major breakthrough in making plastic coated tapered lines. The ability to make a tapered PVC coating on a level inner core gave SA a tremendous economic advantage over its competitors. SA started making lines utilizing this technology in June, 1954.

In early 1955, litigation started between Gladding and SA over the usage of the new SA patented technology—see chapters on Gladding and SA. Consequently, SA developed a second variable coating method that was not in conflict with the first patent. A patent for the second technology was filed on July 28, 1958 and issued in November 15, 1960 (Patent 2,960,063). This second patent ultimately led to an agreement between SA and Gladding where both firms could use both patents.

Others in the line manufacturing industry were also working on developing variable coating thickness technology. Robert Beebe, in behalf of Soo Valley Company in Esterville, Iowa (part of Shakespeare), filed a patent application on December 27, 1954 for a "Fly casting line with tapered cellular waterproof plastic coating." This patent application was filed less than a year after Martuch's application. Beebe's invention was also a process for the application of a tapered coating on a level core. Beebe was issued Patent 2,862,282 on December 2, 1958 (roughly two years before Martuch's patent was issued). Of interest was the fact that Beebe used an additive to the PVC coating called Foam Chemisol to aid in the formation of gas bubbles in the coating.

By the early 1960s, the long era of making tapered braided cores was effectively over because the new variable thickness coating technologies were available.

The early 1950s use of air in the braided line core and air and gas bubbles in the coating for flotation were major advancements. Unfortunately, they did not totally solve the line flotation issue. There was only so much air that could be retained inside a plastic coated line. Additionally, the size, distribution and amount of air bubbles tended to vary widely in the manufacturing process which, in turn, created new issues. The line manufacturing industry was looking for a new way to

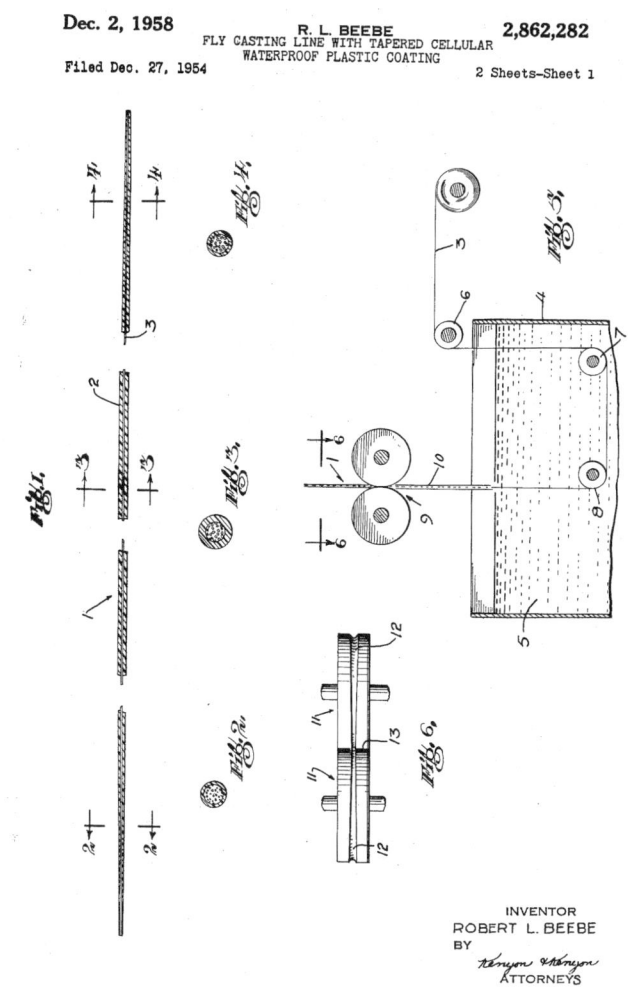

BEEBE PATENT—FILED DECEMBER 27, 1954

make plastic coated lines float better.

The answer came from the oil industry. In 1951, and again in 1953, F. Veatch and Ralph Burhans working with the Standard Oil Company in Cleveland, Ohio filed patent applications for "A Process of Producing Hollow Particles and Resulting Product." Their patent application showed how to make "microballoons" from film forming materials that were substantially free from holes. This meant that they would float. Another positive feature of microballoons is that they can be made to have relatively high wall strength. As such, they are not easily broken. A patent was issued to Veatch and Burhans on June 25, 1957 for this process (Patent No. 2,797,201).

Microballoons (which are also called microspheres, glass bubbles and glass spheres) are very small, hollow glass balloons that look like fine sand particles. They are used as lightweight fillers and additives. For example, many automotive and aircraft plastic parts contain microballoons to make the parts lighter and thus lower the overall weight of the automobile or airplane. Similarly, microballoon fillers are used in paints and countless other products.

Microballoons are very light. For example, a common grade of microballoons made by Minnesota Mining and Manufacturing Company (3M) is called G18. The 18 in the product designation means that the microballoons have a density of 0.18 which is about 1/5 that of water.[103]

3M MICROBALLOONS (LEFT), GLASS BEADS (CENTER) AND POWDERED TUNGSTEN (RIGHT). EACH SAMPLE WEIGHS THE SAME
Courtesy of Scientific Anglers

At this point Leon Martuch of SA entered again. He recognized that the floating qualities of the lightweight microballoons could be an important enhancement in making floating fly lines. His research showed that by putting three pounds of microballoons into 100 pounds of PVC having a specific gravity of 1.3 would reduce the line coating's specific gravity to 0.95.[104] This meant that a line manufacturer would not have to rely on the problematic use of air or gas bubbles in the line coating and line core to make a line float. Line manufacturers could simply add sufficient microballoons to their plastic line coating material and achieve a consistent floating line. Generally, enough microballoons were added so that a floating line would have a specific gravity of 0.95 or less.[105]

Martuch filed a patent application for adding microballoons to fly line coatings on July 20, 1959 and was granted Patent number 3,043,045 for the invention on July 10, 1962. This patent became SA's second major breakthrough in the development of the modern fly line.

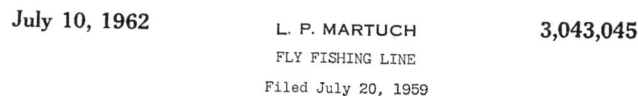

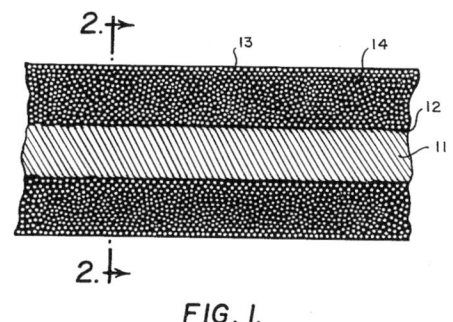

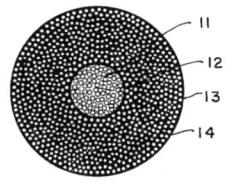

THIRD MARTUCH PATENT

SA then had patents on the two key technologies that the fly line manufacturers had been looking for since WWII. The slow and expensive hand building of braided tapered lines was no longer needed with SA's variable coating patents. The use of microballoons solved the age-old problem of how to get lines to float easily. On the other hand, there were still numerous significant issues that had to be solved over the ensuing 40 years to bring us the fly lines we enjoy today (memory issues, coating-core bonding issues, plasticizer issues, PVC additive issues, and so forth).

Fly line manufacturing had changed from the relatively simple braiding of lines with oil finishes to the manufacturing of fly lines based on complex chemistry and specialty chemical equipment. This change was a struggle for many firms. Since fly lines were only a small fraction of the business of many manufacturers, some decided not to "gear up" to make the new generation of fly lines. They asked competitors to make the new lines for them, which they then relabeled and sold. This, in turn, started a major realignment in the fly line manufacturing industry.

Chapter Four
FLY LINE STANDARDS
The Problem

It always has been important to match fly lines with the actions of fly rods to get maximum casting performance. The historic standard to describe fly lines through WWII was based on the diameter size of the line (i.e., size standard). A micrometer to measure line diameter was a required tool of any serious angler. Anglers talked about their tapered lines in terms of the size components of the various portions of the tapered line (front taper, belly section of the line and back taper).

The historic size standard was as follows:

Line Diameter (inches)	Line Classification
.02	I
.025	H
.03	G
.035	F
.04	E
.045	D
.05	C
.055	B
.06	A
.065	2A
.07	3A
.075	4A

Source: Ashaway 1948 *Sportsman Magazine*

Generally, the size standard had worked well during the silk period of fly lines as most manufacturers made lines roughly in the same way and were all using the same material. When nylon line came into use, the "rule of thumb" was to select nylon lines that were one size larger than the size needed for silk lines. The size standard still held up fairly well.

All of the new changes in synthetic line coatings post-WWII, plus the introduction of new materials for braiding the inner cores of floating fly lines inadvertently created havoc with the historic size standard. Plastic sinking lines aggravated the problem even more. A fly fisherman needing size D floating silk line to get the best performance out of his rod might need a size C floating plastic line and a size E sinking plastic line. All three lines could have roughly the same weight, but greatly different diameters.

Fishermen simply did not know how to buy the right line for their rod anymore as the old size standard was no longer appropriate. A lot of people knew about "The Problem," but what to do about it? It took the fortuitous coincidence of a dedicated line designer, a casting club and a line manufacturer in San Francisco, California to start the necessary changes to develop the New Standard.

The Solution

Myron Gregory was one of the three key components of the solution to the problem. Myron was born in 1908 in Santa Cruz, California (CA). As a youth, he loved fishing—a trait that would be with him all his life. He enrolled in college in 1927 at St. Mary's College in Oakland, CA and graduated with a BS degree in Business Administration in 1931. He had worked at Southern Pacific Railroad (SP) on its commuter trains during college and stayed on with SP after graduating. It was the height of the Depression and jobs were hard to find. Although it was never his intention to stay with SP for his entire career, he did. Myron retired as a freight service conductor in 1974 after 47 years of service. Railroad work was perfect for Myron because it gave him free time to pursue his casting and fishing interests.

Railroad freight work was not for the timid and Myron developed a railroad-toughened nature and ability to take on large challenges. He was a man of letters and his SP work allowed him to write profusely. When he had breaks from his train work, he would type letters. The collection of his writings are now part of the renowned Captain P. Markham Kerridge Angling Collection at California State University in Fullerton, California (CA State Fullerton). Reading them for several hours allows one almost to move himself back into the time when the new fly line standard (New Standard) was being developed. Myron corresponded for decades with a large number of well-known fishermen, as well as fishermen who were not well-known. A small sampling of the more widely known people he corresponded with includes:

Charles Ritz
Jim Hardy
Captain Tommy Edwards
Pierre Creusevant
Arne Schultz
Lee Wulff
Ted Trueblood
Art Agnew
Leon Chandler
Joe Brooks
Mark Sosin
Lefty Kreh
Jason Lucas
Tom McNally
Jimmy Green
Wynn Davis
Hugh Gray
Leon Martuch
Jim Freeman

1957, American casting team, enroute to the international tournament, Kiel, Germany. (left to right) Jon Tarantino, Myron Gregory, Leon Martuch (non-caster) Ben Fontaine and Steve Aleshi.

MYRON GREGORY AND COLLEAGUES IN 1957

So how does a person who works daily on freight trains end up being a colleague with many of the people who were actively involved in competitive fly casting in the U.S. and internationally? It started in 1944 when a friend took Myron to San Francisco's Golden Gate Angling and Casting Club (GGACC), which became the second key component in solving the fly line standard problem. Myron had thought he was a good fly caster until that point, but soon found out at the GGACC that his casting was really not that good.

In many parts of the country, there has been some strain between the fly fishermen who spend their free time on lakes and streams trying to catch fish and the fly fishermen who are involved in tournament casting. The ability to cast long distances is not very important on small brushy streams. Casting is also only one of a large number of skills that a successful fly fisherman has to master in order to be successful in catching fish. Too often lake and stream fly fishermen fail to appreciate the role of tournament casters and casting clubs in the sport of fly fishing. Similarly, tournament casters too often tend to "look down" on the casting skills of most lake and stream fly fishermen.

The truth of the matter is that virtually every major improvement in fly fishing equipment has come from casting clubs that have a membership that is a good blend of tournament casters and practical fly fishermen. Casting clubs are somewhat analogous to today's NASCAR racing where new components and techniques are tried out before going into common usage.

The GGACC is an excellent example of where tournament casters, lake and stream fishermen, and line manufacturers have worked together to improve the sport of fly fishing. The GGACC is a 1933 offshoot of the San Francisco Fly Casting Club, which was formed in 1894 and is the second oldest casting club in America. In 1938, the GGACC got the Work Project Administration of the Federal Government to build casting ponds and associated support facilities in San Francisco's Golden Gate Park. These facilities have been used for national tournaments in 1939, 1950, 1956, 1981, 1993 and 1998. Numerous improvements in rods, reels and lines have been developed at the GGACC. With respect to lines, the use of monofilament for running line (portion of the overall line behind the larger fly line segment) for distance fly casting was developed in 1946. Club members also pioneered the use of shooting heads as a fishing technique. The GGACC also has an excellent web site at www.ggacc.org.

GGACC IN SAN FRANCISCO
Courtesy of William M. Ward

After visiting the GGACC in 1944, Myron Gregory was determined to learn to cast better. As always, he went into the new venture with a vengeance. By 1947, he was beginning to be involved in tournament casting. By 1957, he was part of the America casting team in Kiel Germany at the International Casting Federation tournament casting competition with Charles Ritz, Arne Schultz, and other international casters. In 1954, he was elected the first president of the International Casting Federation (ICF) that had eleven countries as members by 1956. As president of the ICF, Myron was active in a wide variety of activities including trying (unsuccessfully) to get the sport of casting included in the 1960 Olympics. By the end of his competitive casting career, he had held several National Casting Championships and had placed second several times on the international level. Of note, although Myron is normally remembered for his fly casting skill, he also used other types of fishing equipment. At one time, he was the world's distance champion with a spinning rod.

1955 - First meeting of the I.C.F. in Rotterdam, Holland. This photo was taken in the front entrance of the Town Hall in Rotterdam where all the important dignitaries met. Note the red carpet in front.

MYRON GREGORY (CENTER) AT THE FIRST INTERNATIONAL CASTING FEDERATION MEETING IN ROTTERDAM—1955

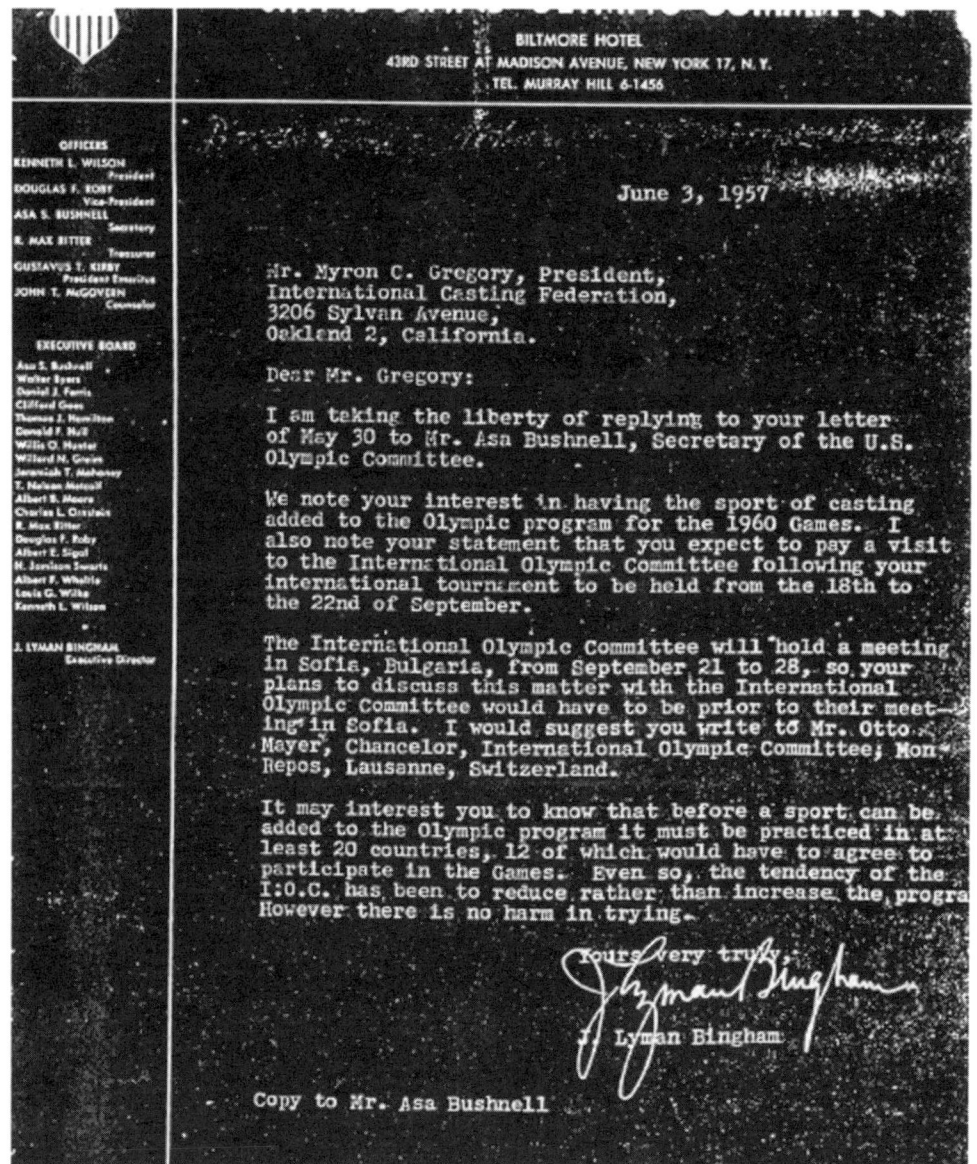

*MYRON GREGORY'S 1957
CORRESPONDENCE WITH THE
U.S. OLYMPIC COMMITTEE*

Myron's preparation for international tournament casting experience required him to learn about fly line construction. The rules allowed each caster to make their own lines, which usually were spliced together from various sizes of level lines. The GGACC was a hotbed of line designers at the time and soon Myron and others were exploring fly line design. The science of line design at this time consisted of the trial and error making of lines. The hope was that the new line would cast better than the last one. Each design was recorded to give a starting point for making the next design. At the beginning, Myron simply went along with the prevailing theories and started his own trial and error experimentation.

As Myron got deeper into line design, he was spending more and more money on buying and building tournament lines based on size—and not getting the results he had hoped. It dawned on him one day that he was really casting a weight, which he called his First Principle. This new truth led him to his Second Principle, which was that the way weight is distributed in a fly line makes it perform as it does. He then correctly guessed that the belly section of a line was its "heart and soul." He soon figured out the various possible combinations of the weight components that could make up a tournament distance casting line.

Lines were quickly made up according to the various possible weight combinations and tested. Myron also had his friends test the various line weight combinations. He came to the conclusion that the best line for tournament casting was one with a continuous taper from front to back. Interestingly, he found that a back taper actually slowed down the line speed and limited the total distance. Soon, Myron's concepts were churning world-wide via his prolific letter writing. Captain Tommy Edwards in London, Arne Schultz in Oslo, Edgar May and his good friend Jimmy Green began to take his line weight concepts and refine them. At one point in time, nearly all the best tournament distance casters in the world were using one of Myron's designs.

Myron and his friends began to think how to take their new knowledge and use it as a basis for a New Standard, which might solve all the confusion associated with fly lines that were being made of new materials. They arbitrarily decided to use thirty feet of line as the portion to use for their weight measurements. Thirty feet was selected for a variety of reasons. One reason was most West Coast fly fishermen were using thirty foot shooting heads. Thirty feet also included the full taper of any line made at the time. It was also arbitrarily decided not to include the level front section in tapered lines in their measurements and that grains avoirdupois would be the weight standard (7000 grains equal one pound).

It is a great tribute to Myron's respect for the fishing public that he simply let everyone know about his new discoveries. Myron was interviewed by Ted Trueblood in a July 1954 *Field & Stream* magazine article that described the work he was doing with developing line designs based on weight. It is also to his credit that he led the fight for a New Standard based on weight rather than size even though he did not need a New Standard personally. He had "written the book" on the new design principles and could have simply gone on with his life ignoring the old standards, which he knew were wrong. His letters convey that he wanted New Standards based on weight for the average fly fisherman who was hopelessly confused with the old size standards.

Of note is that Myron discovered in later years that others had apparently also thought weight was the key factor in line design. Ted Trueblood gave Myron a quote from a book written by a man in England in 1912 saying that weight rather than size was the key factor. Myron modestly said his only contribution was to promote the weight versus size concept to a successful conclusion.

As a world class tournament caster and the first president of the ICF, Myron had enough visibility to move forward his feeling that a New Standard needed to be developed for lines based on weight. In 1958, he proposed a resolution to the National Association of Angling & Casting Clubs-U.S. (NAACC). The NAACC later became the American Casting Association (ACA). He also began corresponding on the same subject with outdoor writer Ted Trueblood and with Jack Holmes. Holmes was Secretary of the American Fishing Tackle Manufacturers Association (AFTMA). Holmes then got Jack Dougherty (President of AFTMA) involved. Jack Dougherty enthusiastically supported the idea. The AFTMA was formerly known as the Associated Fishing Tackle Manufacturers Association. Myron knew that in order to be successful he would need the line manufacturers to cooperate and that he also would need national publicity from the outdoor writers.

In August 1958, the NAACC approved Myron's resolution for a New Standard based on weight. Soon after, the AFTMA formed a committee to evaluate its response to the proposed New Standard. The AFTMA committee members were:

Art Agnew—Sunset Lines (Chairman)
Leon Chandler—Cortland
George Clement—Newton
Jack Dougherty—Gladding
Bob Crandall—Ashaway

Additionally, there were a number of others (in addition to Myron) who were also involved with the new AFTMA committee including:

Leon P. Martuch—Scientific Anglers
Harry Supthin—retailer and tournament caster
Richard Ward—tournament caster and outdoor writer
Ted Trueblood—outdoor writer

At this point, things began to get complicated. Myron and his fellow tournament casters wanted a New Standard primarily for the good of their fellow sport fishermen. On the other hand, the line manufacturers earned their living making lines and naturally were wary of any changes that could upset their current market conditions. Similarly, the rod manufacturers had a stake in the process, as did the retailers. Finally, the outdoor writers defacto had a major vote, as they had tremendous "clout" based upon their readership.

The Gregory Collection of his papers at CA State Fullerton are full of heated exchanges from all of these powerful interests. At first reading, one gets a little disappointed with the various twists and turns in the process (some almost childlike). One of the best known U.S. fly fishing figures opposed the simplified New Standard because he wanted fly fishermen to be at least as intelligent as camera buffs who could use light meters, F stops and shutter speeds for their sport. He, in essence, only wanted high IQ people in the sport of fly fishing. After reflection, these twists and turns were probably the predictable outcome of so many powerful forces and people coming together to work on an issue that could impact their livelihood. Nevertheless, the different viewpoints were reality and needed to be addressed.

At this point, Art Agnew of Sunset Line and Twine Company (the third key component) and others begin to help move the process along. It seems clear from reading the CA State Fullerton correspondence that Myron could not have succeeded on his own in getting a New Standard into common usage. His rough hewn railroad style was not suited to the diplomacy needed to work with the line and rod manufacturers, retailers, outdoor writers, and so forth. In contrast, Art Agnew was just what was needed. He was a respected and broadly liked member of the line manufacturers' "fraternity."

The number of line makers was small in the 1950s and 1960s and although they vigorously competed against each other, they still could meet at the AFTMA and work together on common issues. Art Agnew and Myron teamed perfectly together in this climate with Myron doing the technical research and Art providing the socio-political leadership of the process. Their close proximity to each other in the San Francisco Bay Area also aided the process. As with any committee, some AFTMA participants worked very hard and others less hard. The good news is that the New Standard had several other advocates that were also helping a great deal, including Leon Martuch, Leon Chandler, and Ted Trueblood.

ART AGNEW

Art Agnew's skillful leadership as Chairman of the AFTMA Standards Committee (with significant help from others) resulted in the 1960 AFTMA adoption of a New Standard based on line weight. Leon Martuch, a founder of Scientific Anglers, had never attended an AFTMA meeting until May, 1960. He went to this very important 1960 meeting specifically to support adoption of Myron Gregory's and Art Agnew's efforts.

Well, that should have been the end of the story, but it was just the beginning! Getting a New Standard accepted by the AFTMA was one thing and getting it into use by the general public was another thing. The rod makers also had a stake in the process and they soon were the driving force for the New Standard being expanded to a range of 1-12. It was important to get their support since the New Standard would work much easier if each rod was also marked with it.

The AFTMA New Standard was finally acceptable to all the stakeholders and based on the first thirty feet of the fly line regardless of material density or taper configuration.

NEW AFTMA WEIGHT STANDARDS

AFTMA CODE	WEIGHT IN GRAINS	TOLERANCE RANGE
1	60	54-66
2	80	74-86
3	100	94-106
4	120	114-126
5	140	134-146
6	160	152-168
7	185	177-193
8	210	202-218
9	240	230-250
10	280	270-290
11	330	318-342
12	380	368-392

The majority of the line manufacturers as well as the rod manufacturers were reluctant to immediately change to the New Standard. They wanted to put both the old and new standards on each line and rod. This was understandable, as it would take the nation's fly fishermen some time to understand the New Standard. Promotional material was then developed by the line makers to aid the education of fly fishermen buying their lines under the New Standard.

Then in 1961, a writer in one of the major outdoor magazines reversed his prior support for the New Standard and wrote a major article saying that the New Standard was not needed. This article set off a fire storm of pro-

HOW YOUR CORTLAND "333" FLY LINE MATCHES NEW AFTMA WEIGHT STANDARDS

Basis of new standard .... the weight of the fly line with rod action casts the fly. Performance is poor if the rod and line are not balanced to each other. American line manufacturers in co-operation with the National Association of Angling & Casting Clubs and the International Federation of Casters, prepared these new universal standards. They are based on the weight of the working part of the fly line—the front section. Exclusive of any tip on a taper, the first 30 ft. of line is weighed to determine its category. Now, guesswork in matching the line and fly rod is eliminated.

Code	*Weight	†Range	Code	*Weight	†Range
1	60	54-66	7	185	177-193
2	80	74-86	8	210	202-218
3	100	94-106	9	240	230-250
4	120	114-126	10	280	270-290
5	140	134-146	11	330	318-342
6	160	152-168	12	380	368-392

*Weight in grains. †Allowable tolerances.

IDENTIFICATION SYMBOLS
L — Level DT — Double Taper F — Floating Line
S — Sinking Line I — Intermediate, floating or sinking
ST — Single Taper WF — Weight Forward Taper

CHART FOR CONVERTING FORMER 'LETTER' SIZES TO AFTMA WEIGHT STANDARDS:

333 LEVELS

Old Sizes	G	F	E	D		C	B
New Codes	L3F	L4F	L5F	L6F		L7F	L8F	L9F

333 DOUBLE TAPERS

Old Sizes	HEH	HDH		HCH	GBG
New Codes	DT5F	DT6F	DT7F	DT8F	DT9F

333 ROCKET TAPER

Old Sizes	HDF		HCF	GBF	GAF	GAAF
New Codes	WF5F	WF6F	WF7F	WF8F	WF9F	WF10F

333 BUG TAPER

Old Sizes	GBF	GAF
New Codes	WF8F	WF9F

CORTLAND AFTMA STANDARDS BROCHURE

tests behind the scenes by the many people who had been working on the New Standard for over four years. Fortunately, the New Standard was based on sound technical merit and one article against it did not stop it. In April 1962, Wynn Davis of *Outdoor Life* wrote an important article supporting the New Standard, which reinforced Ted Trueblood's ongoing public support for it in his writings. By the mid-to-late 1960s, the New Standard had generally replaced the old one and dual marking of lines ceased. Change is difficult, though, for some people and organizations. One major line manufacturer did not change its dual markings until 1970—a decade after the New Standard had been adopted.

Myron Gregory was then asked in 1969 by Art Agnew (on behalf of the line manufacturers) to be the independent quality control reviewer for the New Standard. Soon Myron was receiving lines for conformance testing with the New Standard. Myron then got interested in standardizing sink rates for sinking lines, but he did not live to see them adopted.

Even with all of the energy Myron put into working on line standards and design, he always spent lots of time fly fishing. He fished many days every year in the West and also had regular trips to Mexico fishing for saltwater species. He died in 1978.

Mark Sosin summarized his feelings on Myron's work as follows: "No one in this century did more to improve and standardize fly lines than the late Myron Gregory, a long-time tournament caster and master fisherman as well as a close friend. Myron must be credited with urging the American Fishing Tackle Manufacturers Association (AFTMA) to adopt a set of fly line standards that he designed. We have a simplified system today thanks to Myron Gregory."[106]

A lot of other people also worked very hard on getting the New Standard from concept to reality for America's fly fishermen. All those people who helped deserve a great deal of credit and appreciation from the millions of fly fishermen who can now easily purchase a line that matches their rod.

Chapter Five
THE MODERN LINE
(EARLY 1960s THROUGH THE EARLY 1990s)

The new AFTMA standards were adopted in 1960 and were generally in use by the mid to late 1960s. The 1950s inventions of being able to install variable plastic coatings on level lines and the use of microballoons or air bubbles for flotation had created the two essential technologies for the modern fly line. All the key pieces now came together to create the modern fly line.

LINE CORE CONSTRUCTION

Fly line cores during this period were and still are generally made from braided multifilament nylon. Other braided core materials are sometimes used: monofilament nylon, Dacron (polyester fibers), Kevlar, and so forth. Braided Dacron and Kevlar are used when a line manufacturer does not want the core to stretch. Braided monofilament nylon is often used when the manufacturer wants a stiff core for hot weather fishing conditions.

The difference between braided multifilament nylon and braided monofilament nylon is that multifilament nylon is made of fine nylon yarn which, in turn, is made of very small nylon filaments. The earlier generation silk fly line cores can also be thought of as being made of multifilament silk yarn.

Braided monofilament nylon is made by braiding monofilament strands together. One can visualize braided monofilament nylon core line as a braid made of monofilament nylon leader material. Braided monofilament has a rougher surface than braided multifilament nylon. This surface property can sometimes be felt in the smaller diameter sections of braided monofilament fly lines.[107]

*CROSS SECTION OF A FLY LINE
WITH BRAIDED CORE
Courtesy of Scientific Anglers*

THE PVC LINE COATING PROCESS

There are two coating processes commonly used to make fly lines. One is the PVC process and the other is the extrusion process.

The PVC coating process starts with a primer being applied and heat cured to the braided core. This primer step is done to aid in creating a strong bond between the braided core and the PVC coating. The primed core is then passed through a solution of PVC, which also contains the line manufacturer's desired additives. These additives may include: plasticizers, lubricants, heat stabilizers, ultraviolet stabilizers, hydrophobic agents, pigments to provide color, pulverized tungsten (when making sinking lines), and so forth. The PVC and additives are in essence the "recipe" for the synthetic coating that will be applied on the braided core.

The core material, with the PVC coating "recipe" on it, is then generally fed through a variable orifice die and then is thermally cured. The variable orifice die in one form can be thought of as being similar to a camera shutter, which can be made larger or smaller as needed. A combination of increasing and decreasing the size of the die's orifice coupled with the speed of the line going through the die results in the desired line taper.

Leon Martuch's watershed 1960 patent for a "variable strand coating device" accomplished the same variable orifice effect in another manner. Martuch used a pair of mating cams with grooved faces that were linked together so that movement in one caused a corresponding movement in the other. The grooves in the cams had variable depths. Their choreographed movements resulted in an orifice of varying diameter, which produced the tapered line coating.

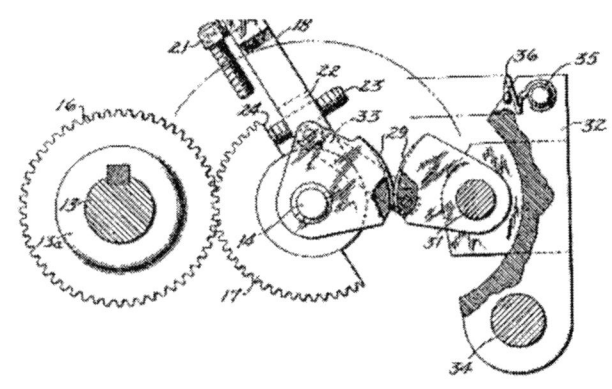

MARTUCH'S MATING CAMS

The original Martuch technology worked fine, but fly lines with different tapers required different groove designs in the mating cams. It was time consuming to change out the mating cams for different tapers. Several line manufacturers found that variable orifice die technologies were easier to use. Berkley's Danny Foote noted the use of camera like "iris diaphragms" in his 1975 patent.[108] Today, computer technology can be linked to a variety of variable orifice die technologies, which allows rapid adjustment in line tapers. Technology now also exists to coat one portion of a single line to float and another portion to sink (i.e., sink tip lines).

THE EXTRUSION LINE COATING PROCESS

Fly lines have also been made over the years by the extrusion coating process. For example, Marathon's Zephyr (polyurethane coating) and Silver Glide (PVC coating) lines in the early 1960s were extruded.[109] Some manufacturers continue today to make quality lines by the extrusion coating process, although many more lines are currently made using the PVC plastisol coating process.

The extrusion coating process is generally associated with using polyurethane as the coating material, instead of PVC. Polyurethane is an elastomer (i.e., rubber compound) and it can be easily and rapidly extruded. Polyurethane (like PVC) is used in countless applications in our modern society such as cushioning for carpet, insulation, footwear, and so forth. Like PVC, polyurethane has a specific gravity that is heavier than water (1.14-1.18) and fly lines using it as a coating material require additional flotation assistance.

Most materials used for synthetic line coatings have advantages and disadvantages when compared with each other. In the case of polyurethane versus PVC, polyurethane is generally more durable and less prone to crack. The extrusion process is also generally faster and less expensive than the PVC process. On the other hand, polyurethane generally has more line memory (maintaining a coiled shape when coming off a reel). Additionally, controlling the amount of material being extruded at any given time is challenging. Finally, polyurethane (like PVC) has bonding problems with some types of core materials.

A 1960s era extrusion process often started with a hollow bullet-shaped device. The core line went through the hollow cavity in the device and the coating material was extruded (normally polyurethane) onto the line as it came out. Next, the core line (with the extruded synthetic coating on it) went through a die to control the maximum coating thickness. A combination of the line speed and the die resulted in the desired taper. The extrusion process was very hot and required a water quench (water cooling) of the coated line as it came out of the die.[110] Extruded fly lines, from the 1960s era, generally did not have the precise tapers associated with fly lines being made by the PVC process.

Over time, extrusion technology for making fly lines improved. In 1990, Paul Burgess of Fly-Fishing Technology, Ltd. in the U.K. was issued a U.S. patent for making extruded fly lines. This patent included several unique features: the use of "haul-off" speed (in addition to line extrusion rate) and laser diameter reading devices that read the diameter of the moving line. These features allowed the creation of precise coating thicknesses and tapers.

Additionally, sodium bicarbonate could be mixed into the raw coating material. It, in turn, released carbon dioxide when heated which formed air bubbles to aid in the line's flotation. Teflon powder could also be added to the raw coating material to aid in distributing the air bubbles and enhancing shootability of the finished line.

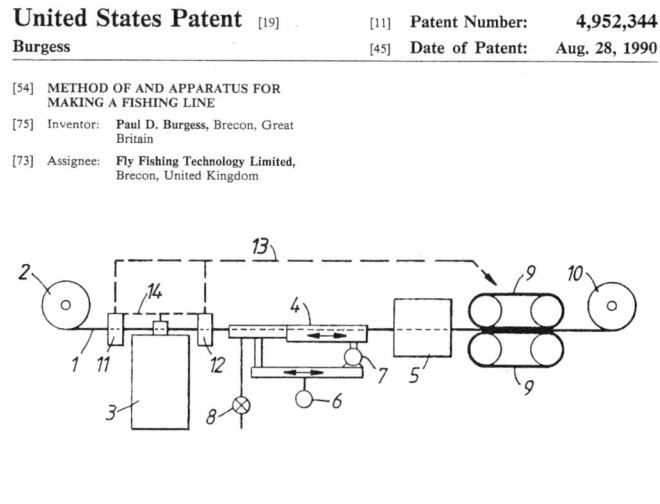

BURGESS PATENT

TECHNICAL PROBLEMS REMAIN

The good news in the early 1960s was that fly line buyers could finally get a synthetic coated line that matched their fly rod's action. The bad news was that there were still significant technical problems that remained. The period between the early 1960s and the early 1990s was devoted to solving these technical problems.

Line memory versus shootability

Line memory (also called coil memory) was a significant unsolved challenge. Plastic by its very nature tends to remain coiled in its last shape. The braided nylon used for the line's inner core had the same basic memory issue. When stored on a reel, a plastic coated fly line's last shape is that of a coil. When removed from a fly reel, the fly line wants to remain in the same coiled shape (i.e., line memory or coil memory).

Some line manufacturers responded to the line memory issue by adding more plasticizers to the coating in order to make their lines less stiff. Making softer lines helped the memory problem, but, in turn, aggravated the ability of the line to be easily cast through the guides of a fly rod (shootability). Softer lines had more sag in the line segments between the guides, which created more friction when going through the guides. More line friction meant less distance for the fly caster. Additionally, if the softer lines were used in hot climates they became even softer and more difficult to cast.

To enhance shootability, other manufacturers took several approaches. One method of enhancing shootability was to put more microballoons in the coating, which created a line with a rougher surface. When a line of this type went through the guides, there was less friction as only the highpoints of the line rubbed on the guides. Less friction meant more casting distance, which was good. The downside was that the fly fishermen felt the rough surface every time they stripped back their line. Over time, these type lines tended to chap the fishermen's hands.

Another method of getting more shootability was to add lubricants to the PVC coating mixture. Line manufacturers had noted early on that the troublesome leaching of plasticizers from PVC actually helped the line's shootability. This was a short-lived condition. Once the plasticizer had leached out

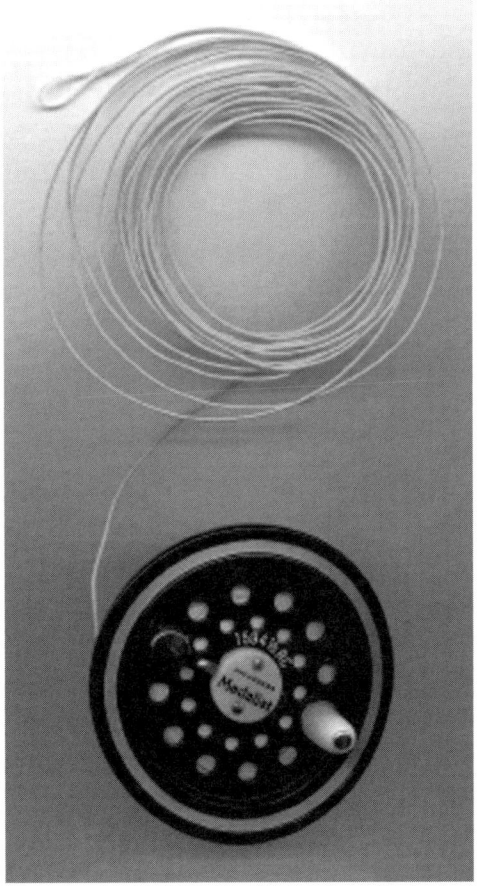

LINE MEMORY

the line, the line was more prone to become brittle and crack under the stress of casting (durability problems). Consequently, much effort was made to keep the plasticizers in the coating while introducing new lubricants that could lubricate the coating's surface. The addition of lubricants had to be done very carefully as uncontrolled lubricants could inadvertently cause coating-core adhesion problems.

Coating adhesion to line core

America's line manufacturers had extensive experience in making braided silk multifilament lines. After the invention of nylon, they used the same technology to make braided multifilament cores for the new plastic lines. Unfortunately, the new nylon lines were less absorptive than silk and some of the plastic coatings did not adhere well to the cores. Adhesion issues are a function of each specific coating formulation and each specific core material. As line manufacturers would change the coating formulations to improve the coating, the new formulation needed to be looked at in light of core adhesion. It was found that solid nitrile elastomers and polyester bulk polymerized urethane elastomers could be dissolved in methyl ethyl ketone solvent and then applied to the line cores.[111] The line cores were then heated to drive off the solvent and any water off the core. Good adhesion was gained after the coating material was then applied and heat cured.

Coating adhesion still remains a challenge when new core materials and coatings are used. Some of the first extruded polyurethane coated lines in the early 1990s did not adhere well to their cores, causing them to be rendered unfishable.

Flotation

The early 1960s use of microballoons solved the problem of how to make PVC lines float easily. Fishermen were so glad to have truly floating lines that they did not initially pay much attention to the pluses and minuses of microballoon usage. The patent for microballoons (also called hollow glass microspheres) was issued in 1957 and microballoon manufacturers using the patent continued to improve the technology associated with their product. This created a situation of dual technology improvement (fly lines and microballoons) that needed to work together.

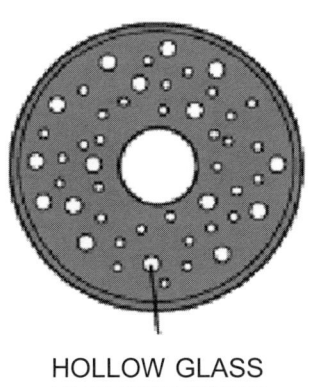

HOLLOW GLASS MICROSPHERES

TYPICAL FLY LINE CROSS SECTION
Courtesy of Cortland Line Company

Microballoons come in many sizes and grades. Unfortunately, one size and one grade will not fit all fly line uses.

The higher grade microballoons are sorted to remove broken microballoons (which sink) and to sort out undersize and oversize microballoons. Microballoons can also be coated to improve coating-microballoon bonding. Large microballoons make lines feel rough and undersize microballoons (having a size of less than about 50 microns) sink even if they are fully intact. This is because the glass shield, which creates the undersized microballoon, is heavier than the air contained inside. Glass has a specific gravity greater than water.

The best lines are made with the higher grades of microballoons, but their cost can be 10-15 times that of the lowest grade.[112] Line manufacturers did not want to put any higher grade of microballoons in their lines than was needed due to this additional expense factor. On the other hand, if they put in too low a grade, the broken microballoons that were part of that grade would make the coating rougher and also cause noise when going through the guides. Broken microballoons also created spherical "dots" on the line coating, which looked like dirt. Additionally, when microballoons were introduced into the coating material, their increased volume also increased the line's final diameter. The larger the diameter of a line the harder it is to cast in windy conditions.

Finally, microballoon usage is especially challenging at the tip ends of floating fly lines. Fly fishermen want their floating line's tip end to have excellent flotation which argues for more and larger microballoons. This, in turn, can lead to an increase in the tip section's diameter. Larger diameter tip sections tend to splash when entering the water.

Given the challenges of using microballoons, other flotation approaches, such as the use of air and gas bubbles in the coating (commonly called frothing), were initially explored. Air is free and air and gas bubbles can provide the same flotation assistance as microballoons. Since air and gas bubbles do not have the glass shield associated with microballoons, their volume impact on lines is also slightly less. Given these positive features, significant effort was put into improving frothing technology for fly lines. In this technology, air is stirred into the coating material being processed or a chemical is used to promote gas bubble generation.

Unfortunately, frothing is a hard process to control as it is very heat sensitive. If the process temperature is too low, less air is available for flotation. Also, the size and distribution of the bubbles is hard to control. Because of these process control issues, most line manufacturers have stayed with the use of microballoons as their principal flotation method. Other flotation aids such as the use of hydrophobic agents in the coating to repel water and, in turn, provide some additional flotation assistance are commonly used.

Starting in the 1990s, there has been renewed interest and success by some manufacturers in finding new ways to design lines that do not need microballoons.

Sinking lines

The new AFTMA standards were designed to standardize the weight of the first 30 feet of a fly line. These new standards, for all intents and purposes, gave the fly fisherman using a floating fly line all the information that was needed to select a line.

As time went on, the increasing popularity of sinking lines created a number of issues that the AFTMA New Standard did not address. Fishermen using sinking lines wanted to know how quickly a line sank, so that they could match the sinking line to the conditions they were encountering.

By the 1970s, most manufacturers were using the numbers 1-3 and in a few cases 1-4 to describe the relative sinking rates of their lines. A Sink Rate 1 line would sink more slowly than a Sink Rate 3 line. The problem was that there was no uniformity of sink rates from one manufacturer's line to another. It was up to the fisherman to know that one manufacturer's sink rate line sank faster or slower than another manufacturer's line with the same numerical sink rate designation.

The AFTMA Fly Line Committee recognized this problem. Myron Gregory, Art Agnew, Leon Chandler and Leon L. Martuch were actively corresponding by 1975 about the need for a sinking line standard. Unfortunately, Myron died in 1978 and did not get to put his full energies into the resolution of this new issue. After Myron's death, James Havstad and others continued writing about the need for sink rate standards.[113] The AFTMA did not take on this issue and line manufacturers continued to individually code their sinking lines. Today, the number of sinking line types for most manufacturers is five or six and they have somewhat different sink rates as measured in inches per second (IPS) when compared to each other.[114][115]

LINE SINK RATES

Cortland (Rocket or WF taper)

Type 1— 1.25-1.75 inches per second
Type 2— 2.50-3.00 inches per second
Type 3— 3.50-4.00 inches per second
Type 4— 4.25-5.00 inches per second
Type 5— 5.25-6.00 inches per second
Type 6— 6.25-7.00 inches per second

Scientific Anglers (Uniform Sink)

1.50-2.25 inches per second
1.75-2.95 inches per second
2.50-3.50 inches per second
4.00-5.00 inches per second
4.50-6.00 inches per second
SA makes a Type 6 in Wet Cel series with 5.50-8.00 IPS

The relative sinking rate and effective depth for fishing can be seen in this SA graphic.

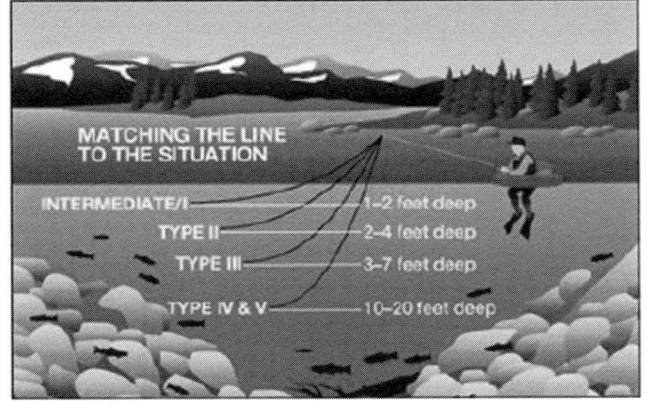

LINE SINK RATES
Courtesy of Scientific Anglers

Other confusion occurred as line manufacturers introduced more and more sink tip lines, which had different sink rates depending on the taper design and tip weighting. Line manufacturers also developed technology that made the tip section of sinking lines more dense than the belly section. This eliminated the belly section sinking faster than the tip section which caused the tip section to bow upward during its descent. The phenomenon of a tip section bowing upward during its descent is believed by many fishermen to cause a decrease in the detection of some fish strikes.

In practice, the lack of standardization of sink rates between manufacturers is not too big of an issue for most experienced fly fishermen. Most fly fishermen simply use inches per second as a reference point for their line selection. Lack of standardization is a more challenging issue for new fly fishermen. Unfortunately, there has been little interest by the fly line manufacturers in developing uniform sink rate standards given the ever increasing complexity of the issue arising from new tapers and line designs.

ADDITIONAL NON-TECHNICAL PROBLEMS

In addition to technical problems, there were a number of equally challenging non-technical issues that the fly line manufacturers also had to face.

Environmental concerns

The use of powdered lead to provide the additional weight for sinking lines had to be discontinued because of the environmental concerns over the lead. The principal environmental reason for the replacement of lead was worker safety in the manufacturing of lead, and also the use of lead by the workers in making sinking lines. In one sense, lead should not have been much of an issue as sinking fly lines are seldom lost in rivers and lakes. Additionally, the amount of lead used in them is small. On the other hand, every conservation measure helps in environmental improvement. Additionally, fly fishermen have always been very environmentally conscious and the use of environmentally unfriendly materials in fly lines was simply inconsistent with their beliefs. More environmentally friendly metals such as powdered tungsten have generally replaced lead in sinking lines.

DENSITY COMPENSATION
ADDITIVES

SINKING LINE CROSS SECTION
Courtesy of Cortland Line Company

Declining numbers of trout and salmon led to "catch and release" practices.

As the Twentieth Century progressed, the historic balance between the natural reproductivity of trout and salmon (and other species) became unbalanced. This was due to a variety of factors: loss of fish habitat due to exploding growth, over fishing, polluted water resources due to industrial releases and so forth.

Society responded to this lack of balance by imposing creel limits and building more fish hatcheries to make up the deficit. New hatchery fish versus wild fish issues then sprung up.

A "catch and release" philosophy was practiced by a few in the first half of the Twentieth Century. This began to change in 1959 when the first Trout Unlimited chapter was formed in Michigan by a group of dedicated fly fishermen (www.tu.org). Wild trout, steelhead, salmon and many other species were simply too important to be caught only once.

America's fishing equipment manufacturers were early supporters of the "catch and release" philosophy because they believed in the concept and good fishing was obviously good for their business. They spent considerable time and money helping the fishing public understand the value of "catch and release."

TROUT UNLIMITED LOGO
Courtesy of Trout Unlimited

Distribution of fly lines

On a historic basis, the majority of America's fly line manufacturers did not have their own sales and distribution staffs which would first sell and then deliver their products directly to the retail dealers with whom the public dealt. Many also lacked the sophisticated business infrastructure to deal with large numbers of customers and all the associated issues: credit checking, accounts receivable, collections, and so forth. Consequently, after a fly line was made it was commonly sold to a "jobber" or "distributor" who, in turn, delivered it to a retail dealer who finally sold it to a fly fisherman. It was not uncommon for a line manufacturer to deal with over 100 local and regional "jobbers" and also with the smaller number of national distributors who provided these essential "middle man" services.

National distribution firms like E. K. Tyron and Shapleigh and Simmons were major factors in the market before and after WWII. E. K. Tyron had its own brand of lines and also distributed other firms' lines. Art Agnew of Sunset Line remembers sending an entire railcar of lines to E. K. Tyron in Philadelphia at one time.[116]

Due to the consolidation of the fly line manufacturing industry after WWII, more and more manufacturers began selling directly to the retail dealer. As such, the role of the local and regional "jobber" was impacted. New national distribution firms evolved such as Maurice Sporting Goods (Maurice), which was started by Maurice Olshansky in 1923. Maurice was originally a sporting goods outlet in downtown Chicago, IL and by 1958, it was in the distribution business. Today, Maurice has distribution centers across the U.S. and in Canada. Maurice provides an essential link to some firms' distribution systems and works with many national fly line vendors and dealers. Maurice has a complete web site at www.maurice.net.

In the 1960s, new, large national retailers such as Wal-Mart and Kmart changed the way the public bought many types of merchandise. The huge purchasing power of these new organizations allowed them to buy large quantities of goods directly from manufacturers and resell them at lower prices. The role of the distributor was impacted under this new distribution system.

The downside of this new distribution system was that the local fishing equipment stores and specialty fly shops did not want to sell the same lines that a person could buy much less inexpensively at Wal-Mart, Kmart, and so forth. The local fishing equipment stores and specialty fly shops are often located near the location where people actually fish and also provide many other essential services. As such, it was and still is important to fly fishermen that these specialty providers remain economically viable.

The result of the new distribution channels was that many local fishing equipment and specialty fly shops would only buy fly lines from manufacturers that did not sell to Wal-Mart, Kmart, and so forth. Some of the larger manufacturers were able to make arrangements with these local specialty providers to sell their higher end products through them, while selling their low end beginner series products through the Wal-Marts and Kmarts of the world.

Some fly line manufacturing firms were unwilling or unable to cope with all the new dynamics associated with their businesses. These firms discontinued manufacturing fly lines as the industry went through a major consolidation.

E. K. TYRON WWII AD

Chapter Six
SCIENTIFIC ANGLERS

Scientific Anglers (SA) was formed in 1945 in Midland, Michigan by Leon P. Martuch, Clare Harris and Paul Rottiers.[117] Leon Martuch was a printer at McKay Press in Midland. He was an avid fly fisherman and was also president of the Anglers Club of Midland.[118] Clare Harris, an engineer, and Paul Rottiers both worked for Dow Chemical Company in Dow's magnesium department. Their partnership was created to manufacturer and sell magnesium fishing rod cases under the Lifetime label. Harris and Rottiers continued to work at Dow, while Martuch left the printing business and worked full time at the new venture. Manufacturing was done in a garage type building behind Harris' home with Martuch's garage being used for the warehouse. The end of WWII resulted in the market being flooded with surplus aluminum and the magnesium rod case business was soon over.

As the rod case business was declining, the three partners developed Hy-Fly, which was a silicone based product to make trout flies float better. They also invented Hy-Line, which was another silicone based product to put on lines as a flotation dressing. Finally, they made Lo-Leader, which was a kaolin clay and detergent product to help leaders sink. Research for these and other new products was done in Martuch's home—often using his kitchen stove.

LEON P. MARTUCH WORKING WITH STOVE
Courtesy of Scientific Anglers

In January 1946, the partners incorporated SA with Martuch and Harris each owning 60 shares with Rottiers owning 20 shares. Total sales in 1946 were $20,012. Paul Rottiers died in 1947 and SA bought back his stock.

In August 1947, SA and B. F. Gladding Company (Gladding) signed a contract in which Gladding got the exclusive distribution rights for Hy-Fly, Hy-Line and Lo-Leader. SA signed another contract in 1951 with Gladding for consulting engineering services. One result under this contract was SA's development of a lubricant called Fibre-Lube, which, when applied to braided casting lines, resulted in fishermen obtaining greater casting distances. A second result was the development of a new coating for level and tapered fly lines. Gladding marketed this coating under the name Cilesto. The new coating was an advancement in coating technology compared to the standard linseed oil-type coatings of the time.

Even though SA's new coating for Gladding represented an advance in coating technology, the making of tapered lines by braiding remained a slow and labor-intensive process. Whereas, level braided line could be made by machine in long continuous lengths, tapered lines were different. To get a tapered line, the braiding machine operator had to stop the braiding machine periodically and either cut or insert a line to decrease or increase the line size. The subsequent waterproofing process was also slow and time consuming.

As America's fly line manufacturers moved to plastic coatings on lines in the late 1940s and early 1950s, the majority of their energy was spent putting a uniform plastic coating on a tapered line. This approach did nothing to address the slow and costly method of making braided tapered lines. SA developed a method to put a tapered plastic coating on a level braided line. SA's Leon Martuch filed for the patent on January 13, 1954 for this new technology and the patent (2,960,062) was issued on November 15, 1960. This new technology was arguably one of the major advances in the history of making fly lines.

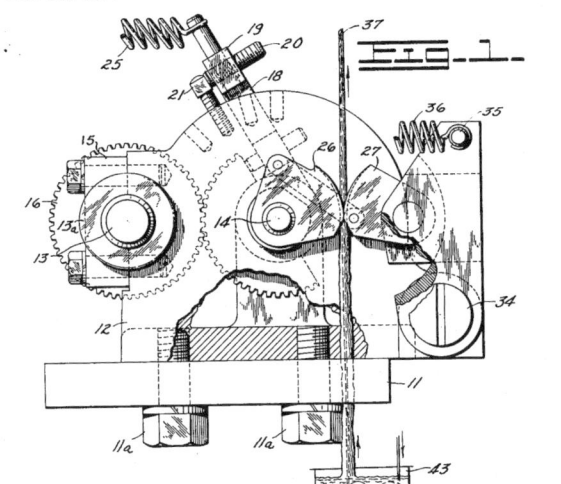

SA 1960 PATENT 2,960,062

SA began to make lines using its new variable thickness coating technology soon after its patent application was filed. This gave SA a great competitive advantage over others in the line manufacturing industry, which were still making tapered lines in the historic way of using a tapered core with a uniform coating. SA's lines had good flotation characteristics due to air bubbles being trapped in the coating. Air bubbles were formed in the plastic coating by the vaporization of moisture from the hollow-braided level core during the tapered coating process. The first lines were sold on June 30, 1954 and were called Air Cel lines. By 1955, there were three series of lines—Air Cel Floating lines, Fisherman Intermediate Density lines and Air Cel Wet Fly lines.

In 1955, SA's new tapered coating technology became embroiled in litigation between Gladding and SA. The dispute was over whether Gladding had the right to an exclusive license to the new technology under a provision of the 1951 Gladding-SA consulting engineering contract. An injunction associated with the litigation required that SA not make lines. Gladding was ultimately successful in the suit (which went on for over two years). SA then developed a second variable coating method that was not in conflict with the first patent. A patent for the second technology was filed on July 28, 1958 and issued in November 1960 (Patent 2,960,063). This second patent ultimately resulted in an agreement being struck where SA and Gladding had access to both of SA's variable coating thickness patents.

In 1959, SA developed a line series called the Air Cel Supreme, which used a new product called "microballoons" to provide additional flotation to the coating. As discussed earlier, microballoons are very small hollow glass balloons that look like very fine sand particles. They are very light (a common microballoon grade has a density of 0.18, which is about 1/5 that of water).[119]

LEON MARTUCH WITH MAGNESIUM FLY ROD CASE AND FIRST GENERATION SCIENTIFIC ANGLERS AIR CEL LINE
Courtesy of Scientific Anglers

Leon Martuch had recognized that the flotation qualities of the lightweight microballoons could be an important enhancement in making floating fly lines. Martuch filed a patent application for adding microballoons to fly line coatings on July 20, 1959 and was granted Patent number 3,043,045 for the invention on July 10, 1962. This patent became SA's second major breakthrough in the development of the modern fly line. SA then had the two key technology components that the line manufacturers had been looking for since WWII. SA was on top of the line world. Business doubled from 1962 to 1964.

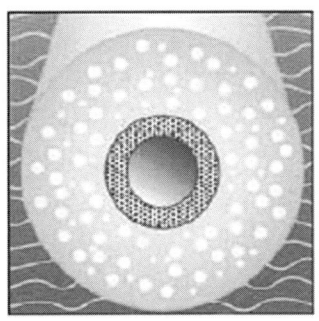

MICROBALLOONS IN A FLY LINE
Courtesy of Scientific Anglers

It is noteworthy that *Field & Stream* magazine recognized SA's patents for variable tapered coatings and the use of microballoons for flotation assistance as being the most important contributions to sport fishing during the 1960-70 decade in the October, 1995 article entitled "A Century of Piscatorial Progress."

SA's management began to change in 1962. Founder Leon P. Martuch was 64 and had been leading the firm for 17 years. He and Clare Harris convinced Leon's son (Leon L. Martuch) to leave Dow Chemical Company and join SA. Clare Harris died later in 1962 and his stock was purchased from his estate and then retired. This left the Martuch family as the sole stockholders of SA. Leon L. Martuch became president of SA in 1964 and began active management of the firm.

SA decided, c. 1962, to sell licenses for all of its technology and also to make private label lines for others. The rationale for this decision was that if SA used its significant technological lead to try and take over the entire market for fly lines that sooner or later someone would find a way to compete aggressively with it. Licensing and private branding for others allowed SA's technology to be used by the whole industry, while earning SA royalties and new clients.

The first client to get a SA tapered coating machine was Cortland in c. 1962. In 1966, a similar agreement was made with Shakespeare's Soo Valley Line subsidiary. Lines were also made in quantity for Ashaway, Sunset, Berkley, South Bend and others under private branding arrangements.

By 1962, the SA fly line series had been changed to Air Cel, Wet Cel and Air Cel Supreme. These plastic coated lines and similar ones from other manufacturers created the need for the AFTMA change in line standards. Leon P. Martuch was very active in helping the AFTMA develop the new line classification standards based on line weight. SA's 1962 lines contained the old letter standard based on size. In 1963, both the letter standard and the new AFTMA weight standard (dual standards) were shown with the lines. Fly lines with the dual markings had small velum inserts in the box that showed the line in pictorial form along with the new AFTMA weight designation and old diameter designation. Dual systems were shown on SA's lines until 1967.

SA AIR CEL LINE (CIRCA 1965)

Scientific Anglers has always provided helpful literature with its products to aid the fisherman in using them. One very helpful item that it provided early-on was a series of charts to help anglers select the correct line for their rod. In 1965, SA's chart listed 381 rods and the correct line for them. By 1968, the chart test list had grown to 508 models.

New lines continued to appear. Bass Bug and Saltwater Tapers appeared in 1963. Wet Cel 1 and Wet Cel Hi-D lines came in 1965 and the Air Cel Shooting Tapers soon followed in 1966. Not every line was a marketing success. SA introduced the Vari-Weight line in 1972. The idea was that the two ends of the line were made for different weight rods. One end worked fairly well with 4-6 weight rods and the other fairly well with 7-9 weight rods. In theory, one line could be used for most types of fishing. The problem was that the public did not like the idea and this line series soon failed.

In 1968, Scientific Anglers also got into the rod and reel business. The J. Kennedy Fisher Company was contracted to make Scientific Anglers' System 4 through System 11 fiberglass rods. The System concept (a phrase coined by Mark Sosin at a 1968 tackle show) was that the fisherman simply took a chart and after determining what kind of fishing he wanted to do, then he selected the System rod, System reel and SA line that was recommended for that use. For example, if a fisherman wanted to fish for trout in small streams using tiny flies and fine leaders, he selected a System 4 rod, a System 4 reel and a DT 4-F line. It was as simple as that. The System rod series retailed for $70 in 1970. Scientific Anglers continued to sell the System rods until 1979. System 100 series reels were built by the Hardy Brothers of England until they were discontinued in 1973.

The decade from 1962 to 1972 was a great one for SA, but the world always continues to change. In 1972, Cortland developed a different coating method and discontinued the use of SA's license. Cortland was also changing ownership in 1972. SA had a chance to buy Cortland, but did not.

In 1973, SA was sold to Minnesota Mining and Manufacturing Company (3M). 3M is a huge company so many people were involved

SA CHART SHOWING RECOMMENDED AFTMA LINE FOR VARIOUS RODS (1976) in the acquisition process. 3M's Lewis " Lew" Jewett was the catalyst for the acquisition.[120] Jewett had joined 3M in 1958 and had started its Leisure Time Products Division. He was an avid fisherman and became a member of the advisory board of Trout Unlimited.

The rationale for the 3M acquisition of SA was that 3M had been selling microballoons to SA and wanted to be more involved in the rod and line manufacturing business. In 1972, 3M had purchased Phillipson Rod and Tackle Company to whom they were selling epoxy resins. 3M's purchase of SA was a period of the "changing of the guard." Leon P. Martuch died on April 28, 1975.

SA continued to grow through continued innovation under 3M's ownership. New lines and products were regularly introduced.

1974—Air Cel Wet Belly Hi-D and Wet Head Hi-D lines were introduced.
1977—Wet Cel Hi-Speed lines were introduced.
1980—Concept lines were introduced circa this date.
1982—Wet Tip Hi-Speed Hi-D and Ultra floating lines were introduced.
1983—Tungsten was used to replace lead in sinking lines.
1986—Monocore lines were introduced.
1986—Silicone was added to Ultra line coatings and phased into other products.
1987—Tarpon and Bonefish tapers were developed.
1987—Backing and leaders were added to the SA product line.
1988—Uniform Sink and Wet Cel V lines were introduced.
1991—Mastery series lines were introduced.
1992—Ultra 3 lines were introduced.

SA SINKING LINE WITH TUNGSTEN
Courtesy of Scientific Anglers

SA ULTRA 3 LINE

3M's innovation also resulted in its staff obtaining new patents for its lines. In 1993, SA's John Stark received a U.S. Patent (5,207,732) for a new coating formulation. This formulation greatly improved the ability for a line to both be durable and have low coil memory (normally associated with soft supple lines) while at the same time good shootability (normally associated with harder and stiffer lines). In 2001, SA's Del Kauss and Bruce

Richards received a U.S. Patent (6,321,483) for a line that further improved shootability and durability through the introduction of Teflon into a new coating formulation.

The technology associated with these patents translated into the Axially Oriented Polymer (AOP) and Advanced Shooting Technology (AST) coatings (introduced in 1998) that have been so popular with SA lines. In 2002, SA introduced the Ultra 4 line series, which is its latest generation of Ultra lines containing AST coating technology.[121]

Bruce Richards, who joined SA in 1976, has become its principal line designer. His 1994 book, *Modern Fly Lines*, is generally considered to be one of the most complete treatments of modern fly line tapers and design.

BRUCE RICHARDS
Courtesy of Scientific Anglers

Specialty line tapers have become an important part of SA's business. Some specialty tapers are offered in the Ultra series of lines with significantly more specialty tapers being offered in SA's Mastery series lines including:

Nymph	Saltwater
Steelhead	Bonefish
Spey	Tarpon
Bass bug	Striped Bass
Pike/Muskie	Bonefish
Windmaster	Billfish
Headstart	Bluewater

While there is no difference in the quality of construction of Ultra 4 versus Mastery series lines, the specialty taper nature of the Mastery series lines requires the sales personnel in the stores selling them to have more background knowledge. SA has set up a program of authorizing certain dealers to handle the Mastery series lines and supporting products. The SA web site (www.scientificanglers.com) gives a list of dealers in the U.S. that handle Mastery products as well as the Professional dealers that handle the traditional SA suite of lines and supporting products.

SA BONEFISH SPECIALTY TAPER

SA is the world's largest manufacturer of fly lines (www.scientificanglers.com). Today, it offers more than 500 branded fly lines and more than 1000 private-label lines. This is an amazing feat for a firm that started its research in the founder's kitchen just after WWII. SA has achieved this lofty status through hard work and scientific innovation, which has greatly improved the modern fly line we all use and enjoy.

Chapter Seven
THE MODERN FLY LINE FROM 1992-2002

The ten years between 1992 and 2002 were exciting ones for fly fishing and fly lines. A popular 1992 movie was responsible for a sudden upsurge in fly fishing interest. Robert Redford brought Norman Maclean's book *A River Runs Through It* to the screen. Millions of people liked the movie about fly fishing and soon there were thousands of new converts to the sport.

Roger Ebert, the film critic, described the movie as follows: *Fly-fishing stands for life in this movie. If you can learn to do it correctly, to read the river and the fish and yourself, and to do what needs to be done without one wasted motion, you will have attained some of the grace and economy needed to live a good life. If you can do it and understand that the river, the fish and the whole world are God's gifts to use wisely, you will have gone the rest of the way.*[122]

POSTER OF A RIVER RUNS THROUGH IT

FLY FISHING BECOMES TRULY INTERNATIONAL

Television was quick to sense the new interest in fly fishing and soon there were numerous shows showing people fly fishing in exotic places (Argentina, Chile, Russia, New Zealand, and so forth). The U.S. stock market was booming and lots of people had the discretionary money to go visit these new places to fly fish. Today, it has been estimated that about one million Americans fly fish at least 21 days a year.[123]

It was also good economic times for other countries. In fact, sport fishing is a major business world-wide. Paumanock Publications estimated the 1996 world fishing tackle market size at 3.2 billion dollars.[124] It was surprising to some Americans that the Japanese and Europeans also liked to fish.

USA	$1.062 Billion* **
Japan	$1.150 Billion
Europe	$538 Million
Asia/Pacific	$211 Million
Canada	$118 Million
Latin America	$37 Million
Rest of the world	$123 Million

*An estimated 50-60 million Americans fish annually.
**Line sales (of all types of lines) are roughly 10% of the total market size.

America's fly equipment manufacturers were aware of these world-wide demographics and aggressively tried to penetrate foreign markets. Fly fishing in Japan and Europe has become as popular as it is in the U.S. For example, there are an estimated 200,000 fly fishermen in Japan today. America's fly line manufacturers have been very successful in marketing their lines to the rest of the world. Today, more than 50% of the fly lines sold world-wide come from the U.S.

FLY FISHING FOR NON-TRADITIONAL SPECIES

As people began to travel more to fly fish, many new species of fish were encountered. Some fish were eager to respond to a fly. Saltwater fly fishing has become very popular in the last ten years (bonefish, dorado, permit, tarpon, billfish, redfish, sea trout, and so forth). Another reason to fish for non-traditional species has been the diminishing stock of U.S. trout and salmon due to pollution and other land use effects. Quality trout fishing is simply harder to find in many places in the U.S.

Fly fishing for non-traditional species encouraged the line manufacturers to create specialty lines and tapers to aid in these new types of fishing. A fly line designed for use in cool mountain streams often does not do well in hot tropical saltwater climates. The line often becomes very limp due to the heat and then does not cast well. Line manufacturers have responded to this condition by designing specialty lines for saltwater fishing in hot tropical conditions. Specialty lines are now also made for a variety of fly fishing conditions: casting in windy conditions, casting large flies, and so forth.

There has also been a dramatic development of specialty tapers for casting to many specific types of fish. There are now specialty tapers available for fly casting to bonefish, tarpon, stripers, billfish, and so forth.

TYPICAL SPECIALTY TAPER

PVC UNDER ENVIRONMENTAL ATTACK

Most fly lines today are still made with PVC coatings. The amount of PVC used in fly lines annually is minuscule compared to PVC usage for other products. In 1992, 6.3 billion pounds of PVC was used in construction (sewer pipes, flooring, weather stripping, and so forth). PVC is composed of chlorine, carbon and hydrogen. The PVC industry is the largest single consumer of industrial chlorine, which amounts to 30% of all chlorine produced.[125]

Environmentalists are concerned about PVC for a variety of reasons: vinyl chloride (a carcinogen) can be produced in the manufacturing of PVC; mercury emissions can occur from the making of chlorine; and common stabilizers (cadmium and lead) in PVC can be toxic.

It is doubtful that PVC will be eliminated as one of the major plastic materials in modern society. We can still anticipate that most of our fly lines will be made with PVC coatings. On the other hand, PVC manufacturing is going to be under continued environmental scrutiny and the fly line manufacturers will have to respond accordingly.

NEW CORE AND COATING MATERIALS

Core materials have continued to change over the years. Single strand monofilament was used at times in the past with varying success for saltwater lines. It is now becoming much more popular because it allows the manufacturing of a clear line. Cortland's new C5 Process takes single core technology a step farther. It has put flotation lumens inside a single "Mono" core in its 555 series floating lines.

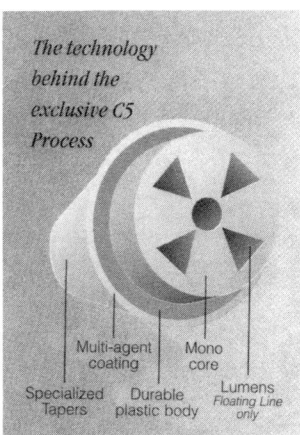

LUMENS IN CORTLAND'S 555 LINE
Courtesy of Cortland Line Company

Although PVC coatings are on the vast majority of fly lines produced in the world, there has been some recent activity in developing other coating and core braid materials. Polyurethane has been used as an extruded coating on some fly lines since the Marathon Zephyr line in the early 1960s. One foreign line manufacturer has been working hard in the last decade to produce high quality polyurethane lines using modern extrusion techniques.

Starting in 1995, some extruded fly lines have also been made with coating materials such as polyethylene copolymers that are lighter than water. As such, they need no microballoons or air bubbles from foaming agents to help them float.[126] Additionally, lighter than water core materials such as gel spun polyethylene (commonly used for baiting casting lines such as "spider wire") are now being used in these polyethylene copolymer coated lines.

The use of new core and coating materials for fly lines is not without its unique technical challenges. Just as with PVC, there are issues with bonding, memory, and so forth, which have to be addressed in the manufacturing of fly lines with new materials.

CLEAR LINES AND "SUPER SMOOTH" LINES

Recent fly line technology has been focused on the issues of presentation and casting distance. Weight Forward (WF) lines have for all intents and purposes taken over the market from the Double Tapered (DT) lines. People have found that a WF line can present a leader and fly as delicately as a DT line can (plus it is easier to cast). The historic advantage of DT lines is that they can be reversed on a reel for additional use. This advantage is becoming less of a factor. More fishermen now simply buy another spool and line rather than take the time to switch the ends of a DT line. Consequently, sales of DT lines have dramatically dropped.

Clear floating lines are now available and they help in some presentations, especially on "spooky" fish species. Braided monofilament nylon cores are white and can not be used to make a clear line. If braided monofilament is used for the core, the weave of the braid is still visible inside the line. In contrast, single strand monofilament nylon is clear and can be used with clear coatings to make clear lines.[127] Bob Goodale of Monic patented a clear fly line in 1997 that had a nylon core and ethylene acrylic acid copolymer coating.[128] Other manufacturers were also similarly active and today, clear lines are available from most major line manufacturers.

MONIC FLY LINES
Courtesy of Flo Tek, Inc.

Greater distance in casting has always been a desire of fly fishermen. In general, the smoother the line coating, the easier it is to make longer casts. Smooth lines also feel better in fly fishermen's hands when they are stripping their line back in. By the early 1990s, some manufacturers began to introduce additional components into or on the coating to enhance casting distance, while not sacrificing reduced coil memory.[129] [130]

Another way to achieve a smoother outer coating is through the use of multiple coatings. Orvis' Earl Duback filed a patent application in 1998 for a line with an outer second coating of acrylic resin bonded polytretrafluorethylene (Teflon) which became the basis for Orvis' super smooth lines. A patent was issued in 2001 and this technology is now used in its popular Wonderline series.[131]

Chapter Eight
THE "NEW MANUFACTURERS"
RIO

Jim Vincent and his wife Kitty Pearson Vincent started Rio in Arizona in the early 1990s. The word "Rio" in Spanish means "river" and also reminded them of a fishing camp that they ran for several years in Costa Rica. In the decade before starting Rio, they both worked full time as outdoor writers and photographers. This allowed them to use their formal art educations. Jim Vincent is a graduate of the San Francisco Art Institute and Kitty Pearson Vincent is a graduate of the Rhode Island School of Design. Their work, before starting Rio, allowed them the ability to travel extensively across the U.S. and also gave Jim time to spend on his hobby of fly fishing. Jim has always been a very active steelhead fly fisherman and early on made his own personal fly lines. He spliced various line segments together to get the tapers and designs he wanted.[132][133]

Rio originally sold leaders and tippet material, much of which was made by a manufacturer in Australia. In 1992-1993, Rio moved to Idaho and by 1994 it started researching how to manufacture its own fly lines. Jim Vincent's background as a writer allowed him access to a wide number of people knowledgeable in the making of fly lines. This was very helpful in Rio's planning process. Early Rio lines were made to its specifications by a major manufacturer. By December 1997, Rio made its first fly lines. The 1998 line series was its first full year of production.

Rio uses core material made by others and a PVC coating process to make its fly lines. Its production equipment utilizes a computerized process to control the line tapers. Rio is known for its extensive research before making a new series of lines, which includes the development of sophisticated tapers to achieve the desired results. Line materials used vary depending on the intended fly line usage. For example, saltwater lines utilize single strand monofilament and braided monofilament core materials with stiffer coatings, which allow them to work better in hot climates. Conversely, for coldwater usage, nylon multifilament braided core material is used with a soft, self-lubricating coating.

RIO LONGCAST FLY LINE

RIO QUICKSHOOTER FLY LINE

Jim Vincent's art background fosters a willingness to try and develop "out of the box" line taper designs and Rio offers a wide selection of these specialty lines. Rio has developed a significant market position in a very short period of time and has an excellent web site at www.rioproducts.com. This web site has a unique "Questions and Answers" feature, which allows prospective line purchasers to research a line series before buying it.

AIRFLO—U.K.

Airflo's lineage began in Great Britain circa 1974 when Paul and Sue Burgess founded a mail order catalog business to sell fly fishing and fly tying materials. They used the name Sue Burgess for the firm. The Sue Burgess brand of fly tying threads and other fly fishing equipment soon became one of the leading brands in the U.K. and Europe. In their catalog business, Paul and Sue Burgess bought and resold PVC technology based fly lines from a number of U.S., U.K. and European manufacturers. In the early 1980s, Paul Burgess decided he wanted to build his own fly lines using different materials. He began extruding fly lines with a polyurethane coating.[134]

In 1989, Paul applied for a U.S. Patent for his technology and on August 28, 1990 was issued Patent 4,952,344. This patent has several unique features in addition to the use of polyurethane for the coating material. These features include:

- laser devices to provide line thickness control,
- the introduction of materials such as sodium bicarbonate to create air bubbles in the coating (microballoons were not used),
- PTFE (Teflon) addition to the coating material and the use of Kevlar for the core material,
- the application of two coating layers on the line.

BURGESS PATENT

Given the development and use of all this new technology it was not unexpected that some of the early lines had characteristics that needed improvement. Adjustments were soon made and Airflo lines proved that polyurethane extruded lines can perform just as well as PVC based lines. New technology continued to be introduced. Airflo was one of the pioneers in the use of Tungsten as a replacement for lead in sinking fly lines. It also was one of the early firms to develop density compensated lines. Density compensation stops the problem of sinking tips, or full sinking lines from sinking in a curve. With density compensation, the tip sinks at the same speed as the body. This helps produce more strikes, provides precise depth control, and better strike detection.

Airflo's fly line series over the years (approximate dates shown) includes:

1987—Super+. This line was arguably the first ever polyurethane line containing Teflon in the coating with a non-stretch Kevlar core;

AIRFLO SUPER+ LINE

1987—Prelude series. This line had the same coating as the Super+ on a twisted nylon core;
1987—XLS series. This line was also a low stretch model;
1992—7000ts series. This line replaced the Super+ line series;
1992—5000ts series. This line replaced the XLS line series;
1992—3000ts series. This was a budget series line;
1994—Gold series. This was its new "top of the line" series;
1997—SP series. This series included its clear floating lines;
1999—Polyfuse series. This was a new series of lines that used Polyfuse technology and includes the popular 7000 series.

Airflo's Polyfuse technology allows it to co-extrude two layers of coating on a fly line. The inner layer is softer and contains the flotation and other key coating additives. The outer layer is harder and slicker which aids in longer casts.

POLYFUSE TECHNOLOGY LINE

On the commercial side of the business, Iain Burgess (the son of Paul and Sue) in 1991 founded a firm called BVG. Originally, BVG was formed to produce corporate videos and then it went into software distribution in 1994.[135] Although not fishing based, BVG had many of the same management components that Airflo did (catalog sales, distribution, accounting, and so forth). Consequently, in late 1995, BVG and Airflo merged to create BVG-Airflo. This allowed much greater efficiency as dual management components were no longer needed. Iain Burgess was selected to head the merged firm and Paul Burgess serves as vice chairman.

The merged firm continues the businesses of both of its historic components with good success. It has been listed on the Welch Fast Track 50 list of rapidly growing companies. In 2002, it was awarded the Welsh Innovation and Entrepreneurial Company of the Year Award for its category of firms. Airflo also has an excellent web site at www.bvg-airflo.co.uk. It is located near a trout river in the scenic Brecon Beacons area of Wales in Great Britain. Airflo has become a significant factor in fly line manufacturing. It now distributes its fly lines in over 25 counties world-wide and also builds fly lines for other firms under private branding arrangements.

AIRFLO'S GARETH JONES (SALES DIRECTOR) AND RICHARD WOTHERS (PRODUCTION DIRECTOR)

MONIC

Flo Tek, Inc., the parent company of Monic, was started in 1990 in Boulder, Colorado by Bob Goodale. Bob Goodale is a Chemical Engineer who early in his career worked with Firestone when it was making PVC plastisol resins. He subsequently worked for General Electric and Arco Chemicals. Over time, he gained a broad understanding of the chemistry and engineering properties of a wide range of materials. In the 1960s, he went into business for himself and invented a product that is used in sophisticated laboratory equipment. He also invented another product that is used by the biotechnology industry. Both of these products became very successful and allowed Bob the means to more actively pursue his hobby of fly fishing.[136]

MONIC'S SCOTT KOZLOWSKI AND BOB GOODALE

Bob Goodale, as a Chemical Engineer, was intrigued by the fact that fly line technology was generally based on using nylon core and PVC coating components. Both of these materials are heavier than water and need microballoons or air bubbles to make them float. He felt that it might be possible to make a fly line using core and coating components that were lighter than water. If this could be done, there would be no need for additional flotation. Starting as a hobby, this quest to make fly lines from new materials turned out to be a long road of experimentation and ended in the formation of Monic. He put together a team of researchers in c. 1978, that began experimenting with materials for new lines. The challenge to make a line from new materials proved to be very complicated. The first commercial Monic lines were sold in 1995—17 years after the start of the research journey. The trademark name chosen for Flo Tek's lines is Monic and it reflects its scientific approach to line manufacturing. Monic is a term used in advanced mathematics.

All of this research effort resulted in the filing of a patent application on May 31, 1994 for a clear floating fly line. A patent was issued on May 6, 1997 for this invention. This new fly line had a ethylene acrylic acid copolymer coating that was light enough to compensate for the heavier than water nylon core and gave the overall line a specific gravity of less than 1. Thus, no additional flotation aids were needed. Monic made these lines using an extrusion process. Another positive feature of these lines was their clear nature, which allowed for improved presentations to wary fish species such as tarpon, permit and bonefish.

The Tropical Clear floating fly line was the first line produced under its new patent. It was designed to be used at temperatures above 65 degrees F in order to minimize reel memory. A Cold Water Clear floating line series soon followed as did the Tropical Light Blue floating fly line, which had a gel-spun polyethylene core fiber-rather than a nylon core. Gel spun cores have very little stretch and, as such, lines using them for cores have very high breaking strengths.

Monic continued its research and the All-Weather Clear series was introduced in 2001 to replace the Cold Water Clear line series. This new line was more durable and allowed nail knot splices to attach both leader and backing. It has a gel spun polyethylene core and a polyethylene copolymer coating. In 2002, the All-Weather Skyline series was introduced. It is translucent in the air, but it provides contrast in the water to aid the fisherman in seeing it.

Monic continues to look for new ways to build extruded fly lines out of new materials. It has been issued a second patent and has applied for a third patent. It has an comprehensive web site at www.monic.com, which shows its line series.

MONIC LINES FOR 2002
Courtesy of Flo Tek, Inc.

NORTHERN SPORT FISHING PRODUCTS, LTD.—CANADA

Northern Sport Fishing Products, Ltd. (Northern) was formed by Bob Armstrong in c. 1971 in Rockwood, Ontario, Canada. It subsequently moved to its present location—Guelph, Ontario. In its early years, Northern was also known as Northern Tackle and Northern Stag. The ownership of Northern changed in 1990 and Richard (Rick) Tramer and Al Fergusson bought the firm.[137]

RICK TRAMER AND AL FERGUSSON

Northern has had a long history of making entry level fly lines and private label fly lines for large general retailers in both Canada and the U.S. This market segment has been essential to fly line development, as there has always been a demand for lower cost fly lines. An individual's view of what constitutes a good fly line has always been predicated to a great extent on what type of line he can afford. Many fly fishermen have used Northern's fly lines that were sold under another firm's name without ever knowing who actually made the lines.

Even though Northern lines are generally aimed at the lower cost point segment of the fly fishing market, they are still made of high quality components. Its braided inner core comes from two of the oldest commercial braiding firms in the U.S. Northern's microballoons and PVC coating material also come from major manufacturers that serve the fly line manufacturing industry.

Northern also sells its own fly lines under the Aquanova label. The word Aquanova means water and new. Northern markets these lines as "a premium fly line without a premium line price." Its lines have generally had a fairly rough coating finish. Northern is currently in the process of manufacturing smoother finishes on its lines. Some of its high-end series now have Teflon in the coating to aid in durability and smooth line feel.

Northern's current line series includes:

- Point 75 Premium line series—this is Northern's flagship line with a very low specific gravity of 0.75 (water is 1.0), which gives these lines excellent flotation characteristics;
- Point 85 Premium line series—this line series is similar to the Point 75 series, but has a specific gravity of 0.85;
- Aquanova 1.6 Premium sinking line series—this is a weight forward sinking line series with sink rates of 2.0-4.0 inches per second (IPS);
- Sink Tip Premium series—this sink tip line series comes in sink rates of 1.75-4.0 IPS;
- 99 Floating Aquanova line series—this standard line series comes in level, DT and WF configurations;
- Brook Trout line series—this level line is an inexpensive entry line series.

In addition to manufacturing fly lines, Northern sells a wide variety of other line products including: lead core line, fly line backing, braided casting line, ice fishing line, and slingshot hunting line. It has a complete web site at www.flyline.net that shows the range of its products.

AQUANOVA LINE

Chapter Nine
SPECIALTY LINES

TEENY

The Teeny Nymph Company (later renamed Jim Teeny Incorporated) was started by Jim Teeny in 1971 in Oregon. When Jim Teeny was a junior in high school in 1962, he invented a very successful trout fly. Like most avid fishermen, the way he made the fly was kept a secret. When he completed his education, he owned and operated a neighborhood movie theatre for six years. He then decided to see if he could make a living selling his fly (which now is known world-wide as the Teeny Nymph). Teeny started his fly fishing tackle business in 1971 and filed for patents on the fly. He was subsequently issued patents for the fly in 1974 (Patent 3,821,862 and Design Patents 229,750 and 233,751).

Jim Teeny was an active winter steelhead fly fisherman and became frustrated with the normal 30 foot long shooting head. He thought the normal shooting head was too long; so he took 3 feet off each end, which shortened it to 24 feet. This length was easier to cast, easier to pick up and required less clearance to cast. Although the shortened head was an improvement, there were still problems with the various line components that needed to be spliced together to make the shooting head system work (e.g., knot between the running line and shooting head, hinge effects, and so forth). Teeny got the idea of making a seamless fly line with a shooting head and running line components. In the late 1970s, he contacted a major line manufacturer to see if they would build a seamless running line-shooting head fly line for him. He was rebuffed on the basis of the technical problems that would be encountered. Teeny persevered and in 1983, he was able to get a major manufacturer to build his seamless line on an exclusive basis. This line series became the now famous T Series lines with a 24 foot sinking section and 58 foot floating running line.[138]

The T series comes in different grain weights for the sinking section (130-500 grains) and is identified by its grain weight. T 200 lines have a 200 grain sinking portion (head). All T series lines have a level running line portion and a 24 foot sinking portion which is also level (level to level configuration). The idea behind not tapering the sinking head was to have the head sink evenly.

The T series lines also has what is now a Teeny trademark of using different colors for the running line portion of the seamless lines. T 200 line have a white running line and a brown sinking head. The T 300 and T 400 lines have orange and yellow running line portions respectively, but the same brown colored sinking head. A fly fisherman can easily tell what weight his line is by simply looking at the color of the running line. The color change also helps identify the point of change from the running line to the sinking head.

United States Patent [19]
Teeny

[11] 3,821,862
[45] July 2, 1974

[54] **FLIES AND METHODS OF MAKING SAME**
[76] Inventor: **Jim A. Teeny,** 915 N.E. 108th, Portland, Oreg. 97220
[22] Filed: **June 20, 1972**
[21] Appl. No.: **264,626**

[52] **U.S. Cl.** 43/42.25, 43/42.53
[51] **Int. Cl.** **A01k 85/08**
[58] **Field of Search** 43/42.25, 42.53

[56] **References Cited**
UNITED STATES PATENTS
1,009,363	11/1911	Winnie	43/42.25
1,388,156	8/1921	Allen	43/42.25
2,034,832	3/1936	Raycraft	43/42.25
2,093,585	9/1937	Woodhead et al.	43/42.25
2,575,248	11/1951	Clark	43/42.25 X
2,618,094	11/1952	Shindler	43/42.53 X

Primary Examiner—Robert Peshock
Assistant Examiner—Daniel J. Leach
Attorney, Agent, or Firm—Klarquist, Sparkman, Campbell, Leigh, Hall & Whinston

[57] **ABSTRACT**

Forwardly extending butt portions of barbs of a tail feather from a Chinese pheasant are bound by a thread to the rear portion of a shank of a hook and are closely wound forwardly on the shank to form a nymph body. The barbs are bound to the shank slightly ahead of the closely wound body and the free end portions are folded back and the thread is wound thereover to hold them in downwardly and rearwardly extending positions to form legs. Then, for a smaller fly, the thread is wound into a head, or for a double fly, a second group of barbs are secured to the forward portion of the shank in a like manner to form a second body with legs after which a head is formed.

13 Claims, 8 Drawing Figures

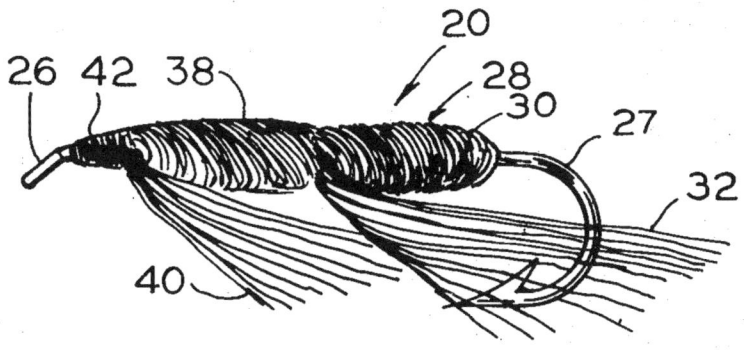

PATENTED TEENY NYMPH

T 200 SERIES LINE

Since Teeny's first lines in 1983, a wide range of additional sinking and floating fly lines are being made to Jim Teeny's specifications. This includes the popular TS series, which has a 30 foot sinking head and a 70 foot running line and the Professional floating line series. There is a complete web site at www.jimteeny.com, which shows the full range of Teeny lines, flies, rods and other fishing accessories.

ROYAL WULFF

Lee and Joan Wulff are arguably the most famous couple in the history of American fly fishing. Lee Wulff was born in Alaska in 1905. He was educated as a Civil Engineer at Stanford University and then went to Paris, France to study art. He became a skilled artist and writer. Additionally, his fishing exploits were legendary until his death in 1991.[139] Joan Wulff won numerous International and National fly casting titles between 1937 and 1960. She is generally acknowledged as one of America's best fly casting instructors.[140]

Royal Wulff started in 1982 in New York as a mail order business selling things that Lee Wulff or Joan Wulff had invented, written about or endorsed. They had been under contract with Garcia Corporation immediately prior to starting Royal Wulff. While at Garcia, Lee Wulff had designed the popular "long belly" fly line for them. Soon after starting Royal Wulff, it became evident that it needed a unique retail product to support its catalog based business.[141]

Lee Wulff then developed the concept of making a fly line with a continuous taper similar in shape to that of a tapered leader. In profile, the front portion of the fly line has a slender triangular shape. The line becomes ever wider in its portions farther away from the tip until a point where the line has a short reverse taper and joins a shooting line segment. A patent application was filed on July 26, 1982 for this design and Patent 4,524,540 was issued on June 25, 1985. Royal Wulff then contracted with a major line manufacturer to make fly lines for it in accordance with the specifications in the patent.

TRIANGLE TAPER LINE

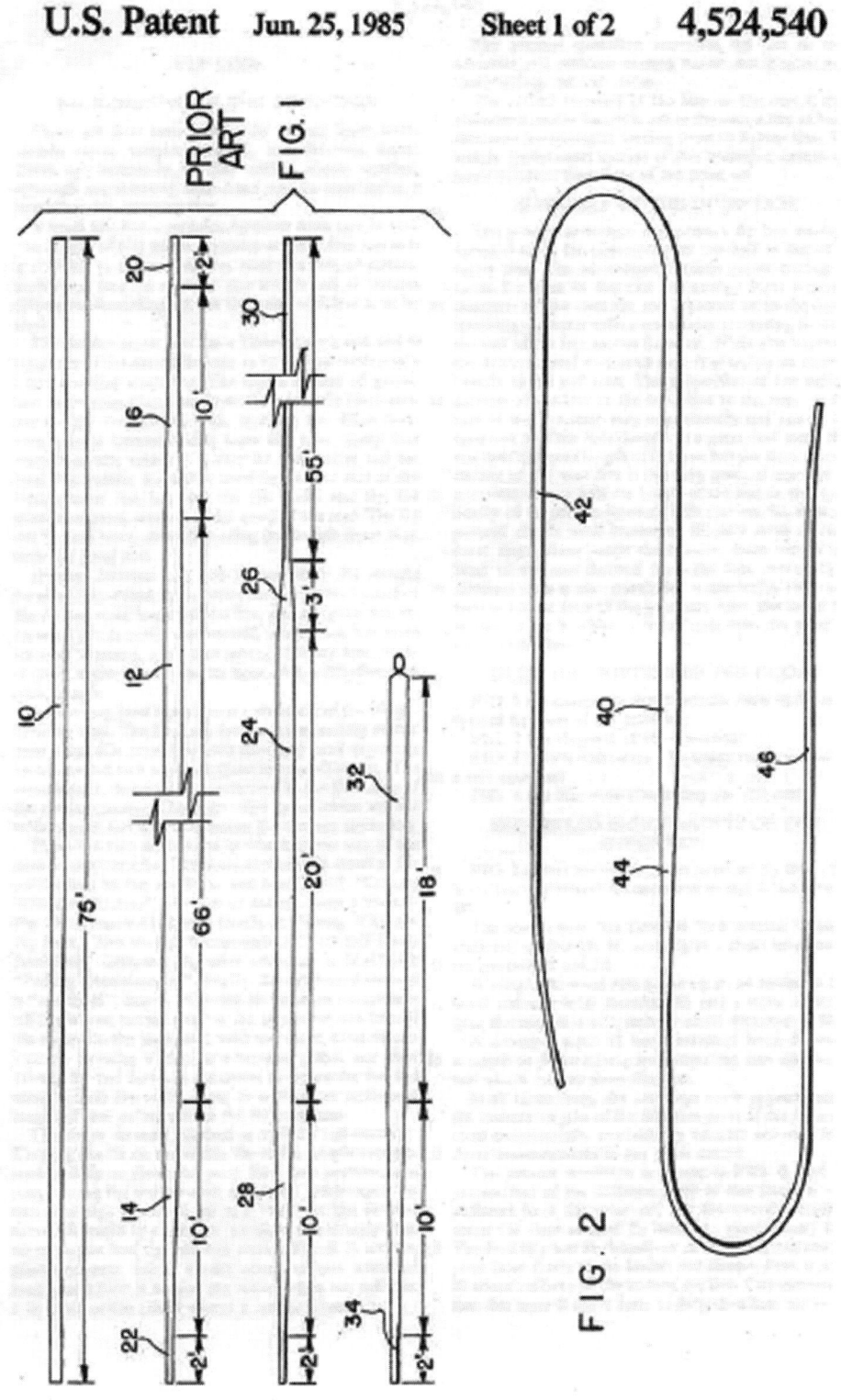

DRAWING FROM THE PATENT FOR THE TRIANGLE TAPER LINE

The name Triangle Taper was given to the patented design and it remains the trademark design of Royal Wulff's products. Most of Royal Wulff's lines use variations of this design. Triangle Taper lines have a continuous taper in the first 27-80 feet of the line depending on the model. They utilize the mechanical advantage of having heavier line portions of the line turning over lighter line portions. This design has proved especially good for roll casting, where it is considered one of the premier line designs. The design also promotes delicate delivery of flies since the heavier portions of the line remain farther from the end of the line.

One of the challenges of using Triangle Taper lines on very long casts comes at the point where the wide belly of the line narrows down in about 2 ½ feet to join the running line. First time users sometime experience a hinge effect in their cast, but with a little practice they soon make the long smooth casts they desire.

Joan Wulff has designed a very popular line series called the Joan Wulff Signature Line. This weight forward line has a 32 foot head, an 8 foot handling line segment with the remaining portion of the line being the shooting line. There is a color change between the head portion of the line and the remainder of the line, which helps as a reference point for better casting.

Royal Wulff provides a full suite of both fresh and saltwater fly lines that it has made to its specifications. These lines embody the high level of commitment that Lee and Joan Wulff have given to the sport of fly fishing. Royal Wulff has a comprehensive web site at www.royalwulff.com, which shows all the products and services it provides.

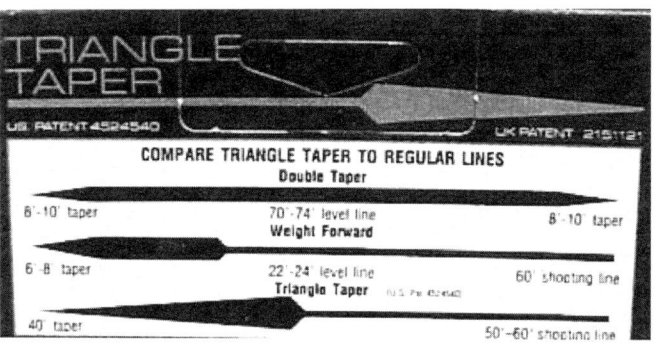

TRIANGLE TAPER LINE COMPARISON

JOAN WULFF SIGNATURE LINE

THE "MODERN SPECIALTY RETAILERS"
ORVIS

Charles F. Orvis was born in 1831 in Manchester, Vermont. The Manchester area has a long history of having excellent fishing on the nearby Battenkill River. Young Orvis liked to fish. When he reached adulthood, he went into the tourist business by opening a successful hotel. One of his hobbies was building rods for himself and friends. In 1856, he used the profits from the hotel business to form the C. F. Orvis Company (Orvis) to manufacture fishing rods. The rod business prospered and became well established by the Civil War. Rod makers of the Civil War era were using a variety of woods in making their rods. By the late 1800s, Charles Orvis and the rest of the rod industry had evolved into using split cane for the making of fly rods.[142]

Charles Orvis' first big technology breakthrough came in 1874 when he received a patent on what now is considered by many to be the forefather of most modern fly reels. He died in 1915, and was succeeded in the business by his sons, Robert and Albert. Of note is that Charles' daughter, Mary Orvis Marbury, was in charge of Orvis' fly production and wrote *Favorite Flies and Their Histories*, which is one of the most significant landmark books in fly tying literature.

CHARLES ORVIS
Courtesy of The Orvis Company, Inc.

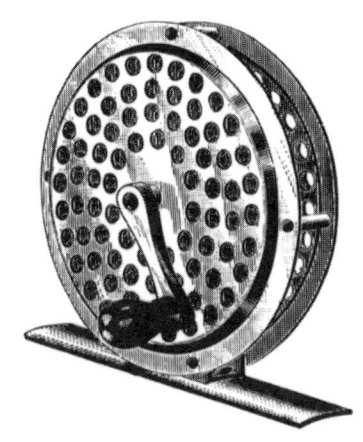

ORIGINAL ORVIS REEL
Courtesy of The Orvis Company, Inc.

The Depression severely hurt Orvis and by 1939 it had only two employees. It was sold at that time to Dudley C. Corkran. Soon after the sale, WWII started and Orvis switched to war production. It made bamboo ski poles for U.S. ski troops. Following the war, another major Orvis breakthrough occurred when Wes Jordan and other Orvis employees perfected a process

FLY, CASTING & TROLLING LINES

Newton Nylon

Orvis Silk

Ashaway Nylon

ORVIS LINES (1960)

of impregnating split cane rods with Bakelite. This allowed for making a much more durable and moisture-resistant rod. A patent was issued in 1950 for the process.

In addition to its historic rod and reel sales, Orvis has a long tradition of selling fly lines. For many years, it primarily sold fly lines made by others through its catalogs.

1952—Orvis was selling Newton and Ashaway silk and nylon lines.

1955—Orvis was selling Gladding Aerofloat nylon and Bub-L-Ett nylon lines, as well as Newton and Ashaway silk and nylon lines.

1957 and 1960 catalogs featured an Orvis brand oiled silk line that was made to its specifications. In 1957, it cost $13.00-$15.00 depending upon the taper. Additionally, Orvis was still selling Newton, Ashaway and Scientific Anglers Supreme series fly lines.

1962—Orvis was still selling its Orvis brand oiled silk line, as well as lines made by Newton, Ashaway, Gladding and Scientific Anglers (SA). The SA lines were the Supreme series as well as the Wet Cel sinking line series.

Dudley Corkran sold Orvis in 1965 to Leigh Perkins.[143] Leigh Perkins was able to transform Orvis from a relatively small firm in 1965 ($500,000 in annual sales) to a large firm by 1992 ($200,000,000 in annual sales). In 1992, Leigh Perkins turned the running of Orvis over to his sons, Perk and Dave. Perk Perkins is currently the CEO and Orvis continues to grow.

(L to R) David Perkins, Leigh H. Perkins, Perk Perkins

LEIGH PERKINS AND SONS
Courtesy of The Orvis Company, Inc.

In 1967, Orvis was selling more and more Orvis branded lines made to its specifications.

A floating series was featured in its 1967 catalog that sold for $14.50. Cortland and SA lines were also featured in the same 1967 catalog.

In 1969, Orvis was also selling a silk line made for them by Cumberland-Aylestone, Ltd. (Cumberland) in England. Cumberland's King Eider silk line series were internationally known. Additionally, the trend toward selling more and more of its own Orvis brand of lines continued.

ORVIS 1969 FLOATING (TOP) AND SILK LINES

By 1971, Orvis was primarily selling only its own brand of lines. As specialty lines became popular, they were added to Orvis' catalogs in the ensuing years.

The explosive growth under the leadership of Leigh Perkins resulted in changes to Orvis' historic business model. Orvis began to change the historic balance between items it had made to its specifications by others versus items such as rods that it made itself. In 1990, Orvis bought Gokey Boot Company, which had been in business since 1850. This was soon followed in 1993 when it bought British Fly Reel. This gave Orvis the ability to make its own fly reels. Orvis was vertically integrating into more and more manufacturing. It wanted to have more control over the products it sold.

This new corporate direction also impacted Orvis' fly lines. Orvis' Jim Lepage and Earl Duback, a consultant to Orvis, began experimenting with ways to make fly lines more slick.[144] Increased line slickness would result in better and longer casts. Their research was done in Earl Duback's garage and resulted in a patent application being filed on September 25, 1998 and a patent being issued on January 2, 2001 (Patent 6,167,650). The patent covered the use of a second very slick coating on fly lines. This second coating contains polytetrafluoroethylene contained in an acrylic resin binder. Orvis now buys fly lines made to its specifications that have the manufacturers' first coating. These lines come in lengths of up to 150 lines. Then, Orvis applies its patented second coating. This dual coated line series is the popular Wonderline series.

ORVIS WONDERLINE

The Orvis Company is one of the oldest mail order companies in the U.S. and it is one of the best known brands of quality fly fishing equipment. It sends out over 30 million catalogs a year and also has 35 retail stores and over 500 dealers in the U.S. Orvis has an excellent web site at www.orvis.com and its history since 1965 is described in detail in Leigh Perkins' recent book, *A Sportsman's Life*. Quality goods and sporting equipment coupled with superior service have always been part of the Orvis tradition.

L.L. BEAN

L.L. Bean, Inc. (L.L. Bean) was founded by Leon Leonwood Bean (Bean), an enterprising 40-year old Maine outdoorsman and entrepreneur. Bean had become tired of coming home with sore wet feet from the heavy woodsman's boots of his day. In 1911, he created the Maine Hunting Shoe, which had a lightweight leather top and all rubber bottoms. L.L. Bean was officially started in 1912. Within a few years, the Maine Hunting Shoe had become a big success and L.L. Bean began selling other hunting and sports equipment and apparel. For years, L.L. Bean would sell no outdoor product that Bean did not personally test. Initially, L.L. Bean products were available only through the mail, but in 1917 L.L. Bean opened a showroom in Freeport, Maine. The firm continued to grow. In 1951, L.L. Bean initiated 24 hours a day, 365 days a year service to anyone appearing at the Freeport store. Of interest is there are still no locks on the doors of the Freeport store.[145]

L.L. BEAN BEHIND A MOUNTAIN OF MAIL
Courtesy of L.L. Bean, Inc.

LEON GORMAN
Courtesy of L.L. Bean

L.L. BEAN AS A YOUNG MAN
Courtesy of L.L. Bean, Inc.

Mr. Bean died in 1967 at the age of 94 and was succeeded by his grandson Leon A. Gorman. In 2001, Leon Gorman stepped up to the role of chairman of the board and appointed Chris McCormick as president. McCormick joined the firm in 1983 and is the first non-family member ever to hold the position of president.

L.L. Bean has a long history of having manufacturers make fly lines to its specifications and then selling them in its stores and through its catalogs.

*1933—It was selling a 75 foot enameled line that cost 50 cents.

*1937—It was selling its Bean's Four "X" silk double tapered line for $5.00 and it was selling its 25-yard Double Duty level silk line for $1.10.

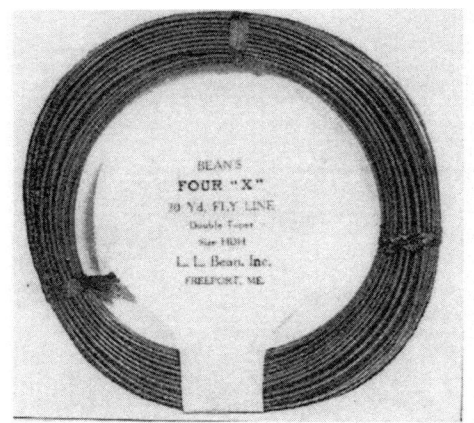

BEAN'S FOUR "X" LINE (1937)

*1945—It was selling level and tapered "LL" lines, with a level line costing $2.65 and a tapered line costing $5.35.

BEAN'S TAPER ""LL"" LINE (1945)

*1950—It was selling its level silk "LL" series and also selling a silk Torpedo Taper series.

*1955—It was still selling its silk "LL" and Torpedo Taper series.

*1960—It was selling its nylon Bean's Sinking Line and its Bean's Floating line. The Bean's Sinking Line cost $6.95.

BEAN'S SINKING LINE (1960)

*1965—It was selling its nylon Double L floating lines that had a vinyl finish and also selling its nylon Bean's Sinking Line.

By the 1970s, L.L. Bean was still selling its own brand of lines as well as others from Scientific Anglers and Cortland. It also began to move away from the longstanding "LL" series fly lines by introducing new line series. In the mid-1990s, it introduced its popular Guide Quality Series (GQS) and Quest series (for beginning fly fishermen). This was followed by the Smooth Power Transfer (SPT) series, which remained until 2000. In 2001, L.L. Bean discontinued selling lines under its own brand name and now sells Scientific Angler lines through its catalogs.

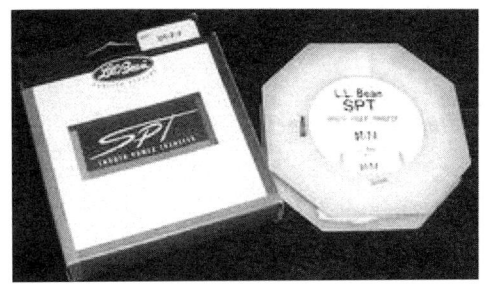

L.L. BEAN SPT LINE

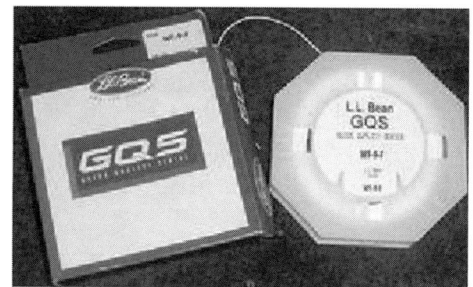

L.L. BEAN GQS LINE

L.L. Bean is an important part of America's outdoor heritage and has always provided quality products at a fair price—along with legendary service to support its products. Its fly lines have always met its high standard of excellence. L.L. Bean's marketing impact is huge as it sells over 16,000 items in more than 80 separate catalogs. In 2001, L.L. Bean sent out the amazing number of 227 million catalogs to its customers. In addition to its historic Freeport store, L.L. Bean now has other retail stores in Virginia, New Jersey and Maryland—as well as numerous factory stores across the U.S. It also has an excellent web site at www.llbean.com.

CABELA'S

Cabela's was founded by Dick and Mary Cabela in 1961 in Chappell, Nebraska (NE). Dick Cabela's family had a furniture store in Chappell. While Dick was on a business trip to a furniture show in Chicago, he encountered a person selling flies. He bought some flies. He then advertised them first in a Casper, Wyoming newspaper and subsequently in *Sports Afield* magazine, in 1962.[146]

As people would buy the flies, Dick and Mary would send along a mimeographed catalog of the other products they had added to their product line. This generated more orders and the cycle repeated itself. This new direct mail business worked well and in 1963, Dick's younger brother, Jim, joined the business.

CABELA'S AD IN SPORTS AFIELD (1962)
Courtesy of Cabela's

JIM AND DICK CABELA (1999)
Courtesy of Cabela's

The growing business required more and more space. In 1969, Cabela's moved to a vacant John Deere building in nearby Sidney, NE. By 1986, the building and showroom was too small because of Cabela's rapid growth. A second showroom store was opened in Kearney,

NE. Growth continued and today there are eight Cabela's stores. Cabela's sends out 75 million catalogs a year to all 50 states and 120 countries. As such, it is a major factor in fishing equipment sales.

One of Cabela's catalogs is a very complete fly fishing catalog. It contains products, including fly lines, from a large number of quality manufacturers. In 1996, Cabela's began having fly lines made to its specifications and branded as Cabela's lines. These Cabela's fly lines are sold in parallel with fly lines from major manufacturers. They are also included whenever a person buys a Cabela's "combo" package containing a Cabela's rod, reel and fly line.

There are two series of Cabela's fly lines. One is the Prestige series, which is designed for beginner to intermediate fly fishermen. Prestige series lines have a loop type line to leader connector to aid a beginning fisherman in attaching leaders. Each line also comes with two colored segments to aid a beginning fisherman in knowing when to cast again.

The second series of Cabela's fly lines is the Prestige Plus lines, which have improved flotation characteristics and more sophisticated tapers to allow for longer casts. These lines are designed for the more advanced fly fisherman.

CABELA'S PRESTIGE PLUS LINE

It is clearly a point of great pride that Dick and Mary Cabela were able to start their now vast enterprise on their kitchen table. Dick and Mary with Jim Cabela's subsequent help, have guided their firm to become one of the largest suppliers of recreational equipment in the U.S. Cabela's has a complete web site at www.cabelas.com which, along with its fly fishing catalog, provides fly fishermen convenient access to quality fly fishing equipment.

CABELA'S PRESTIGE FLY LINE

BASS PRO SHOPS

John L. Morris started Bass Pro Shops in 1972 in Springfield, Missouri (MO). John was a tournament bass fisherman and wanted to find a consistent source of the specialized fishing gear he needed. When he could not find the source he was looking for, he asked for some shelf space in his father's liquor store. He stocked the shelves with the specialized gear bass fishermen desired. By 1974, Bass Pro Shops was sending out catalogs; and by 1984 it had started building its famous Bass Pro Shops mega store in Springfield, MO. In the ensuing years more mega stores have opened and there are now a total of 15 nationwide—with more on the way.[147][148]

BASS PRO SHOPS STORE LOCATIONS
Courtesy of Bass Pro Shops

JOHN L. MORRIS
Courtesy of the Missouri Sports Hall of Fame

Bass Pro Shops sponsors special events for its customers and the 10 day Spring Classic at its flagship Springfield, MO store attracts over 400,000 visitors each year. Bass Pro Shops also sends out in excess of 34 Million catalogs annually which include over 30,000 items. Its huge store sizes plus its significant catalog sales program make it a major factor in fishing equipment sales, including fly fishing equipment.

Bass Pro Shops has developed a fly shop inside of each store called the White River Fly Shop. Each White River Fly Shop sells White River fly fishing equipment (including fly lines that Bass Pro Shops has made for it according to its specifications). The White River brand of fly equipment is aimed at the beginner to intermediate fisherman. For the more advanced fly fisherman, Orvis fly fishing equipment is also available.

WHITE RIVER CONSERVATIONIST FLY LINE

Bass Pro Shops has also started a division called American Rod and Gun, which allows small independent local businesses to buy White River brand fly fishing equipment at wholesale prices. Another new venture of Bass Pro Shops is X-Treme Angling, which plans fishing trips all over the world for Bass Pro Shops' customers. The growth of Bass Pro Shops in the last 30 years has been huge and has brought quality fishing equipment to a large number of fresh and saltwater anglers. It has an excellent web site at www.basspro.com.

Chapter Ten

"TAKE CARE OF YOUR FLY LINE"

BY J. LEON CHANDLER

The modern fly line is a remarkable product that has evolved over a period of several decades by utilizing a blend of space age materials, efficient taper designs and manufacturing know-how. The fly line you buy today can be expected to provide you with many hours of pleasant fishing—but a fly line is not indestructible. By following a few reasonable precautions, you can insure that your line will last longer.

The appearance of small radial cracks in the finish coating will offer the first visual clue that a fly line is reaching the end of its useful life. Cracks occur because the plasticizers within the finish formulation have migrated or moved. The role of plasticizers can be compared to the milk in bread dough—in simplest form, they are the liquids that hold solids together and provide the suppleness that is so important in fly line performance. Once cracks appear and water is admitted, further deterioration is fairly rapid. Plasticizer migration will occur naturally over a period of time. The chemical process can be accelerated if the surface of the line is exposed to solvent base chemical substances (such as are found in most brands of insect repellent, suntan lotion and gasoline), to excessive heat, or prolonged exposure to the ultraviolet rays of direct sunlight.

It is a well-known fact that most insect repellents are murder on fly lines, they are equally destructive to rod finishes. If it is necessary to use liquid repellents, be especially careful about handling your line with repellent residue on the palms of your hands. Use the back of the hands to spread repellent to the neck and face.

Keep your floating fly line clean! In normal use, even on clean water, microscopic particles of dirt and debris will adhere to the surface of a floating line, adding weight that may eventually overcome the natural buoyancy built into the line itself. Because it contains a thinner coating of the buoyant finishing material than does the larger diameter body, the tip section of a tapered line will begin sinking first—an indication that it should be cleaned. What is the best method to follow in cleaning a floating line? Opinions vary. Some manufacturers include cleaner saturated felt pads in the line package, with the recommendation that the working part of the line be wiped with the cleaner pad each time before starting to fish. In addition to removing surface residue, the pad will leave a film of lubricant on the surface to assist the line in moving efficiently through the rod guides. Another manufacturer recommends washing the line with a mild soap and water solution and wiping dry with a soft, clean cloth. Regardless of the method used, clean your floating line frequently and you will be rewarded by a line that will give you better performance and considerably longer life.

Heat. Never ever leave a line-filled fly reel on the dashboard or rear ledge of an automobile parked in the hot sun. The level of heat buildup from the sun coming through the windshield or rear window can literally cook the line and start internal plasticizer migration. Visible cracks may not occur immediately, but the damage will have been done.

Most anglers are acutely aware of the importance of frequently checking rod guides for wear induced sharp areas that will scuff or cut the surface of a fly line. Most however, overlook the fact that the line guard area of the reel actually gets more wear from stripping off line than do the guides. A sharp projection on the reel line guard can slice and ruin a line in short order.

Some fishermen use methods of retrieving and controlling line that do little to prolong the life. For example, the procedure commonly referred to as the "hand twist" retrieve can place an unusual amount of stress on that portion of the line that is handled. Gradually, the portion continually squeezed and stretched will break down.

Fly line manufacturers are frequently asked to identify the life expectancy of their products—an impossible question to answer because of the variables involved. Much depends upon the conditions under which lines are used, the degree of care given and of course the amount of time a line is in actual use. One manufacturer suggests that except for the most avid angler the average user can expect his line to perform well over two seasons. Another suggests that if his lines are used under normal conditions and given normal care, one can expect to log 200 to 300 hours of actual use. Beyond that time he should expect that the end of useful life is being reached.

Most experienced fly rod anglers agree that the fly line is just about the most important part of the equipment because it plays such an important role in the effective presentation of artificial flies. Your line deserves Tender Loving Care. It will respond by giving you much fishing pleasure.

Chapter Eleven

PRICE GUIDE FOR ANTIQUE FLY LINES

Americans love to collect antique fishing equipment. There is enormous collector interest in antique rods, reels, and lures. In respect to fly lines, the collector community is currently much smaller. This makes fly line collecting a relatively inexpensive hobby and an excellent way to enjoy America's fly fishing history.

So then, what to collect? Where to find it? What to pay for it? There are numerous ways to approach starting a collection. Some collectors focus on a single manufacturer and look to obtain most or all of the lines that the manufacturer has made. Others want to obtain the oldest lines they can find, while others want only silk lines. Others simply want to collect the type fly lines they used in their youth. Finally, some want to collect novelty fly lines and trolling lines such as the one shown below:

The easiest place to find old fly lines is on the Internet. Ebay (www.ebay.com) is a popular Internet site and normally has antique (vintage) lines listed as well as photos of them. Another good place to find old fly lines is through the publications of antique fishing tackle firms such as:

Adams Angling - 1170 Keeler Ave., Berkeley, CA 94708, telephone: 510-849-1324, AdamsAngl@aol.com

Len Codella's Sporting Collectibles Catalog—2201 South Carnegie Drive, Inverness, FL 34450, telephone: 352-637-5454, www.codella.com

Martin Keane's Classic Rods and Tackle, Inc.—P.O. Box 228, Ashley Falls, Massachusetts 01222, telephone: 413-229-7988

Antique fishing equipment shows are another good source for old fly lines. For example, a popular antique fishing equipment show in the western U.S. is the Santa Rosa, CA show. It is usually held in early March and is organized by Red Johnson (telephone: 707-545-6357). Antique shops and estate sales are also good places to look for lines. The search for the great "find" is part of the joy of collecting.

When looking for lines, there are a number of common-sense guidelines. Unused lines with their original box are obviously worth more than similar lines that have been used and do not have their original box. Box graphics are also an important factor. Some lines came in boxes that were truly fishing art, while others came in relatively nondescript boxes. If you are collecting silk lines, look for whether the line is still pliable or whether the waterproofing has "stuck the line all together." Some lines came with pamphlets or other marketing materials that described the line and the company. This type of additional information enhances the value of lines. Normally, lines that can be precisely dated are always more desirable than similar lines that cannot be easily dated.

ENGLISH KING-EIDER LINE WITH EXCELLENT GRAPHICS

For starting collectors, here is a partial list of fly lines that you might want to look for, which have wide appeal. This makes them excellent lines to start collecting, until you decide on what type of collection you want. Once the focus of your collection is made, these lines can either remain in the collection or easily be sold or traded for the type of lines you want to collect.

SILK LINES

1) Ashaway Crandall's American Finish silk lines
2) Ashaway line containers with native American twisted good luck symbols on them
3) Bevin Wilcox Pilot silk lines
4) Cortland Ivanhoe silk lines
5) English Hardy Corona silk lines
6) English King Eider silk lines
7) English Kingfisher silk lines
8) Gladding Trans-Lu-Cent silk lines
9) Gudebrod Fly King silk lines
10) Horrocks Ibbotson Supreme silk lines
11) Horton Kingfisher De Luxe silk lines
12) Marathon Supreme silk lines
13) Newton Streamline silk lines
14) Rain-Beau Hedge 7 Taper silk lines
15) S.A Jones President and Governor silk lines
16) Shakespeare Tru arT silk lines
17) South Bend Excel Oreno silk lines
18) Sunset Arrowhead silk lines
19) Weber Henshall silk lines

NYLON AND SYNTHETIC COATED LINES

1) American Line Company Flex series lines from 1942
2) Cortland 333 lines from 1953
3) Garcia Lee Wulff series lines
4) Gladding Payne series lines
5) Marathon Golden Zephyr lines
6) Scientific Anglers Air Cel lines from 1955
7) Sears Ted Williams series lines

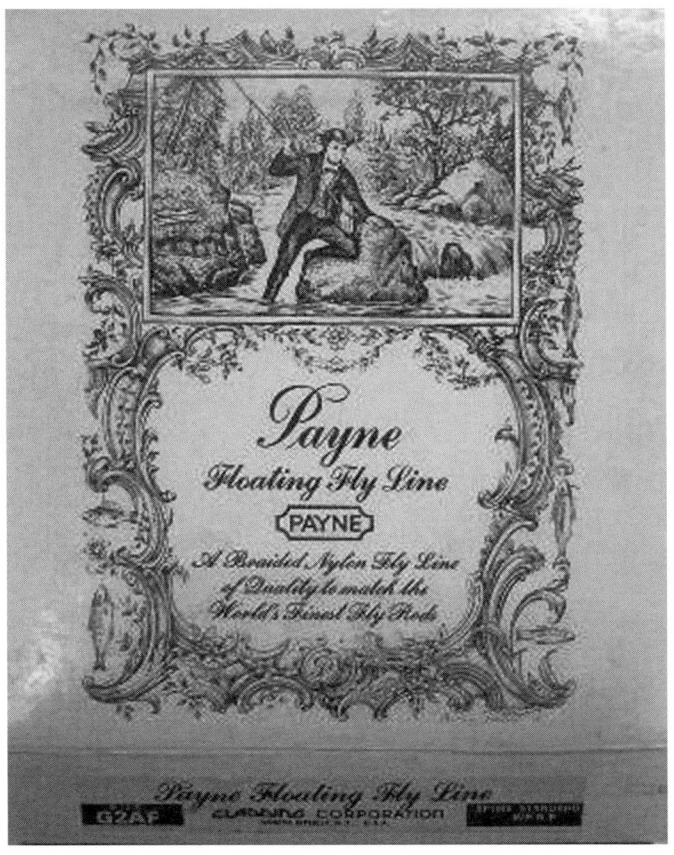

GLADDING PAYNE LINE WITH EXCELLENT GRAPHICS

FLY LINE DRESSINGS

LINE DRYER

FLY LINE CLEANERS AND DRESSING TINS AND FLY LINE DRYERS

There is also a small but active collecting market in antique fly line cleaning and dressing tins (containers). Tins that have undamaged high quality graphics are sought after. It is not uncommon to see an individual tin container selling for $10 or more. Similarly, fly line dryers are another unique item to collect. Some are woodworking pieces of art and sell for up to $100 or more, with even metal ones selling for $25-$50. Again, condition and being able to trace a dryer back to its manufacturer and date of manufacture are key value considerations.

PRICE GUIDE*

Manufacturer	Line Series	Type	Condition	Price	Comments
Ashaway	Crandall's American Finish	Silk	Unused	$65.50	
Ashaway	Fly Sport	Silk	Unused	$65.00	
Ashaway	Nylon	Nylon	Unused	$8.35	
Ashaway	Nylon	Nylon	Used	$1.00	Poor shape line
Ashaway	Silver Knight	Aluminized Line	Unused	$35.01	
Ashaway	XF 100	Nylon floating	Unused	Did not sell at $9.99	
Ashaway	XF-100	Nylon floating	Unused	$5.00	
Ashaway	XF-100	Nylon floating	Unused	$8.50	
Bevin Wilcox	Pilot	Silk	Unused	$103.50	
Bevin Wilcox	Non Kink	Silk	Unused	$12.00	Line stuck together
Cortland	333	Plastic/Nylon	Unused	$10.00	
Cortland	333	Plastic/Nylon	Unused	$14.58	Circa 1963
Cortland	333	Plastic/Nylon	Unused	$34.99	Circa 1953 line (first year made)
Cortland	333	Plastic/Nylon	Unused	$3.99	Small Angler Line
Cortland	333	Plastic/Nylon	Unused	$9.99	
Cortland	Cam-O-Flage	Nylon	Unused	$6.52	
Cortland	Ivanhoe	Silk	Unused	$27.00	
Cortland	Ivanhoe	Silk	Unused	$43.55	
Cortland	Ivanhoe	Silk	Unused	$69.00	
Cortland	Ivanhoe	Silk	Unused	$75.01	
Cortland	Regal Scot	Silk	Unused	$15.50	Box rough
Cortland	Regal Scot	Silk	Unused	$53.00	
Cortland	Say Brook	Enameled Silk	Unused	$41.00	
Cortland	Trophy	Nylon floating	Unused	$9.99	
Cortland	Micro Foam		Unused	2 rolls sold for $2.26	
Garcia	Dick Wolff Autograph	Dacron	Unused	no bids at $9.99	
Garcia	Lee Wulff	Plastic/Nylon	Unused	$2.00	
Garcia	Lee Wulff	Plastic/Nylon	Unused	3 rolls for $12.50	
Gladding	Aerofloat	Plastic/Nylon	Unused	$5.00	
Gladding	Aerofloat	Plastic/Nylon	Unused	$7.60	
Gladding	Aqua Sink	Dacron	Unused	$6.05	

*Actual sales prices from a variety of sources.

Gladding	Cilesto	Nylon	Unused	$19.50	
Gladding	Cilesto	Nylon	Unused	$10.07	
Gladding	Payne-Invincible	Plastic/Nylon	Unused	$250.00	
Gladding	Payne Invincible	Plastic/Nylon	Unused	$95.00	
Gladding	Ripple	Nylon	Unused	$15.51	
Gladding	Super	Plastic/Nylon	Unused	13 rolls for $31.01	
Gladding	Whip Silk	Silk	Unused	$46.00	
Gudebrod	Fly King	Silk	Unused	$71.00	
Gudebrod	Sink-R	Dacron	Unused	no bids at $9.95	
Hardy		Silk	Unused	$33.05	Circa 1920's
Hardy		Silk	Unused	$147.50	
Herter's	Masterweave	Nylon	Unused	$15.50	
Horrocks Ibbotson	Dry Flite	Nylon	Unused	$15.50	
Horrocks Ibbotson	Dry Flite	Nylon	Unused	$19.15	
Horrocks Ibbotson	Dry Flite	Nylon	Unused	2 rolls for $12.49	
Horrocks Ibbotson	HI Float	Plastic/Nylon	Unused	$2.10	
King Eider	English	Silk	Used	$85.00	
King Eider	English	Silk	Unused	$125.00	
Kingfisher	English	Silk	Unused	$92.82	
Kingfisher	English	Silk	Unused	$91.00	
Kingfisher	English	Silk	Unused	$91.00	
Marathon	Perma Float	Plastic/Nylon	Unused	$41.00 for 4 rolls	
Marathon	Nylon	Nylon	Unused	$13.19	semi rough box condition
Montgomery Ward	Sport King	Nylon	Unused	$12.04	
Newton	Airline	Nylon	Unused	no bids at $4.99	
Newton	Brook Trout	Enameled Finish	Unused	$19.00	
Newton	Ghost	Nylon	Unused	$10.49	
Newton	Phantom	Nylon	Unused	$12.49	
Newton	Phantom	Nylon	Unused	three lines for $6.99	
Newton	Huckleberry Finn	Silk-Enameled	Unused	$51.00	
Rain-Beau	Rain-Beau	Silk	Unused	$97.00	H. Schindler & Co. era line

Rain-Beau	Fly Beau	Nylon	Unused	$41.00
S. A. Jones	Governor	Japanese Silk	Unused	$114.05	Year 1938 on label
Scientific Anglers	Air Cel Supreme	Plastic	Unused	$51.00	Early 1960's line
Shakespeare	Nylon	Nylon	Unused	$9.99
Shakespeare	Presidential	Plastic/Nylon	Unused	Did not sell at $4.99
Shakespeare	Wexfloat	Nylon	Used	$10.60
Shakespeare	Wexford	Nylon	Unused	$5.50
Shakespeare	Wonderfloat	Nylon	Unused	$8.28
Shakespeare	Wonderfloat	Nylon	Unused	2 rolls for $10.53
South Bend	Excel Oreno	Nylon	Unused	No bids at $9.00
South Bend	Oreno	Enameled Silk	Unused	$45.00
South Bend	Super Jet	Nylon	Unused	$5.00
Sunset Line	Arrowhead	Nylon	Unused	$16.30
Sunset Line	Arrowhead	Nylon	Unused	$9.99 for 4 rolls
U.S. Line	Golden Spinner	Silk	Unused	$60.50
U.S. Line	Golden Spinner	Silk	Unused	$61.00
U.S. Line	Golden Spinner	Silk	Unused	$66.00
U.S. Line	Westfield	Nylon	Unused	$8.00
Weber	Henshall	Silk	Unused	$95.00
Western Auto	Good Luck	Enameled	Unused	No bids at $7.50
Western Auto	Revelation	Silk	Unused	$36.50

CONTRIBUTORS

Agnew, Art
Arteburn, Joe
Ashmawy, Alaa
Balch, Jim
Balch, Richard
Barton, Kathryn
Basore, Dan
Beckwith, Shirley
Belleville, David
Berescik, Susan
Berry, Herb
Bevin, Stanley
Borgstrom, Lennart
Brindley, Chris
Brookes, Barbara
Brown, Carolyn
Ceder, Ernest
Ceder, Ted
Chandler, Leon
Christakos, Don
Christakos, Nick
Chu, Alan
Coleman, Roxanne
Collins, Louannne
Conner, Don
Cook, Chester
Cottrel, Trish
Crandall, K. C.
Cummings, Doug
Cutter, Vic
Davis, Mark
Dollosso, Art
Dierberger, George
Dietrichs, Tripp
Foote, Dan
Garrett, John
Goodale, Bob
Haering, Bob
Harbison, Nancy
Hoffman, Dave
Hoffman, Elizabeth
Hunt, Nigel
Ibbotson, Ed
Irvin, Tom
Johnson, Dolly
Johnson, Sarah
Jones, Gareth
Jones, Jacinta
Kane, Mary Ann
Karlson, Orrest
Kauss, Del
Kerstein, Bob
Klink, Laura
Knotek, Nancy
Kohn, Jean
Kropf, Valerie Krabill
Krupa, Gail
Landry, Jennifer
Lefkowitz, Mary
LeGrande, David
Lepage, Jim
Lindler, Monroe
Ludwig, Wendy
Malzahn, Monte
Manewitz, Jay
Martuch, Leon L.
Mazurkiewicz, John
McIntosh, Jim
Miller, Diane Horton
Nelson, Rex
Neuland, Marilyn
Norris, Clay
Ogelby, Chris
Ogilvie, Kristine
Paumanok Publications
Perry, Sharon
Phanef, Bernie
Pliska, Sylvester
Price, Bonnie
Prince, Joan
Rajeff, Katherine
Reeder, Kate
Richards, Bruce
Rief, Kay
Rogers, George
Rose, Leslie
Schindel, Mark
Schmidt, Dennis
Schultz, Tommy
Scott, Patricia
Sentura, Michael
Shepherd, Helen
Shuman, Elizabeth
Stadler, Diane
Stanfield, Walt
Stout, Nancy
Sundall, Larry
Tankersly, Larry
Teeny, Jim
Teufel, David
Thomas, Brian
Tramer, Rick
Vincent, Jim
Vincent, Kitty Pearson
Walz, Carolyn
Ward, William
Weber, Robert
Westcott, Judy
Whiteley, Larry
Williams, Jon
Wolff, Dick
Wong, Terry
Yearack, Todd

REFERENCES

1. Victor R. Johnson and Victor R. Johnson, Jr., *Fiberglass Fly Rods* (Colorado Springs, CO: Centennial Publications, 1996)
2. Plaque at the Scientific Anglers booth at the Fly Fishing World Trade Expo, September 12-14, 2002, Denver, Colorado
3. Herman Henkin, *Fly Tackle* (Philadelphia and New York: J.B. Lippincott Company, 1976)
4. AFTMA Fact Sheet developed by Leisure Trends Group, Boulder, CO and released at the Fly Fishing World Trade Expo, September 12-14, 2002, Denver, Colorado
5. http://www.dogsofthedow.com/djdelete.htm
6. Ernest Schwiebert, Trout, (New York: Truman Talley Books-E.P. Dutton, Inc.,1978)
7. Larry Koller, *The Treasury of Angling* (New York: Ridge Press-Golden Press, 1963)
8. Turhan Tirana, *Fly Fishing* (Kensington Books, 1957)
9. Larry Koller, *The Treasury of Angling* (New York: Ridge Press-Golden Press, 1963)
10. Larry Koller, *The Treasury of Angling* (New York: Ridge Press-Golden Press, 1963)
11. Izaak Walton, The Compleat Angler,(London: 1676)
12. Larry Koller, *The Treasury of Angling* (New York: Ridge Press-Golden Press, 1963)
13. Herman Henkin, Fly Tackle (Philadelphia and New York: J. B. Lippincott Company, 1976)
14. Len Codella, *Spring 2000 Sporting Collectibles Catalog* (Florida: 2000)
15. Ashaway Line and Twine Manufacturing Company magazine, *Ashaway Sportsman* 1948
16. A.J. McClane, *Field & Stream magazine,* July 1952.
17. A.J. McClane, *Field & Stream magazine,* July 1952.
18. http://www.vegansociety.com/html/info/info19.html
19. http://scholar.chem.nyu.edu/tekpages/silk.html
20. Henry P Wells, *Fly-Rods and Fly Tackle*, written in 1885 and reprinted by Derrydale Press, 1994
21. John Saunders, *The Compleat Fisherman*, (London, 1724) as shown on http://www.pbagalleries.com/catalogs/curcat216-4.html
22. Edward R. Hewitt, *Hewitt's Handbook of Fly Fishing* (New York: The Marchbanks Press, 1933)
23. http://narvellstrickland1.tripod.com/cottonmillhistory2/index1.html
24. http://www.curlbros.com/cottinfo.htm
25. Edward R. Hewitt, *Hewitt's Handbook of Fly Fishing* (New York: The Marchbanks Press, 1933)
26. http://www.ulsterlinen.com/2.htm
27. U.S. Line Company, *U.S. Lines Catalog Number 109*
28. Interviews with Art Agnew of Sunset Line and Twine Company
29. www.braiders.com/braidingtech.htm
30. http://www.herzog-online.com/en/index.html
31. Rufus Jarman, *Hard to Fool a Fish*, (The Saturday Evening Post, April 23, 1949)
32. Rufus Jarman, *Hard to Fool a Fish*, (The Saturday Evening Post, April 23, 1949)
33. Lee Wulff, *Outdoors magazine* (November, 1948)
34. Lee Wulff, *Outdoors magazine* (November, 1948)
35. Edward R. Hewitt, *Hewitt's Handbook of Fly Fishing* (New York: The Marchbanks Press, 1933)
36. Edward R. Hewitt, *Hewitt's Handbook of Fly Fishing* (New York: The Marchbanks Press, 1933)
37. The Weber Lifelike Fly Company product literature circa 1947
38. Charles E. Brooks, *Nymph Fishing For Larger Trout* (Publisher: Globe Peqot)
39. Charles E. Brooks, *Nymph Fishing For Larger Trout* (Publisher: Globe Peqot)
40. Newspaper article by Wendy Fontaine of The Sun, *175 years of success* (provided by Ashaway Line and Twine Manufacturing Company, circa 1999)
41. Larry Koller, *The Treasury of Angling* (New York: Ridge Press-Golden Press, 1963)
42. http://www.lib.niu.edu/ipo/ihy000452.html
43. Magazine article by Ralph B. Cooney, *A Century And A Quarter Of Leadership* (provided by Ashaway Line and Twine Manufacturing Company, circa 1949)
44. Magazine article, *Textile Age County Club* (Textile Age, August 1937)
45. http://www.pbs.org/wgbh/aso/databank/entries/btcaro.html
46. Magazine article by Ralph B. Cooney, *A Century And A Quarter Of Leadership* (provided by Ashaway Line and Twine Manufacturing Company, circa 1949)
47. Ashaway Line and Twine Manufacturing Company magazine, *Ashaway Sportsman* 1948
48. Leon L. Martuch, *A History of Scientific Anglers from 1945 to 1973* (Personal manuscript written in February 1996)
49. http://www.gudebrod.com/
50. Interviews with David LeGrande of Gudebrod
51. Correspondence with Nancy Stout with Cortland Line Company
52. http://www.chronofhorse.com/features/99/whip_city.html
53. Interviews with Chester Cook of U.S. Line Company
54. Interview with Rex Nelson of Western Filament and information from http://users.acsol.net/~wfi/history.html
55. Interviews with Art Agnew of Sunset Line and Twine Company
56. Interview with Walt Stanfield
57. http://www.geocities.com/Heartland/Hills/1496/book/bibook2.htm
58. Larry Koller, *The Treasury of Angling* (New York: Ridge Press-Golden Press, 1963)
59. Newspaper Article in the Stevens Point Journal (March 21, 1985)

REFERENCES

60 1921 *Penny Press* newspaper article furnished by the East Hampton, CT Public Library
61 http://216.239.35.100/search?q=cache:leAjPX_Q_nUC:www.kaleden.com/articles/2055.html+bevin+bells&hl=en&ie=UTF-8
62 Interviews with Judy Westcott and Stanley Bevin
63 http://home.att.net/~slowsnap/history12.htm
64 http://home.att.net/~slowsnap/history12.htm
65 Material provided by Eloise Shuman-Town Historian of Otselic, NY
66 Material provided by Shirley Beckwith-Chenango County Historian's office.
67 Rufus Jarman, *Hard to Fool a Fish*, (The Saturday Evening Post, April 23, 1949)
68 *Pathfinder News Magazine* (Washington, DC: April 20, 1949)
69 Newspaper Article from *The Evening Sun* dated February 4, 1972
70 Material provided by Barbara Brookes of the Utica Public Library
71 Material provided by Ed Ibbotson
72 www.south-bend.com/history.html
73 Interviews with Leon Chandler of the Cortland Line Company
74 Leon L. Martuch, *A History of Scientific Anglers from 1945 to 1973* (Personal manuscript written in February 1996)
75 Newspaper Article from the South Bend News Times dated March 28, 1929
76 Interview with Monroe Lindler
77 Material provided by the Akron-Summit County Library, Akron, Ohio
78 Interviews with Leon Chandler of the Cortland Line Company
79 *Rod & Reel Magazine*, January/February 1984
80 Material provided by Mary Ann Kane of the Cortland County Historical Society
81 Material provided by Nancy Harbison of the Phillips Library
82 Newspaper article by Rocco Palladino in the Cortland Standard (May 6, 1959)
83 Information supplied by Nancy Stout with the Cortland Line Company
84 Interviews with Danny Foote and Clay Norris
85 Material provided by Mary Ann Kane of the Cortland County Historical Society
86 Interviews with Danny Foote
87 Interviews with Vic Cutter
88 Interview with Lennart Borgstrom
89 Interview with Dick Wolff
90 Material provided by Dyanne Horton Miller
91 Material provided by Jay Manewitz with the Bristol Public Library.
92 James V. O'Gara, *The Shop That Sells Dreams* (Coronet, September 1957)
93 *Caterer to the outdoor man* (Business Week, December 16, 1961)
94 Jeff Hedtke and Vernon L. Ferch, *Herter's of Waseca* (Minnesota Waterfowler, date unknown)
95 R.V. Gaddis, *The Flying Fisherman* (New York: Pocket Books, 1967)
96 Rufus Jarman, *Hard to Fool a Fish*, (The Saturday Evening Post, April 23, 1949)
97 http://www.si.edu/lemelson/centerpieces/whole_cloth/u7sf/u7materials/nylondrama.html
98 Magazine article by Ralph B. Cooney, *A Century And A Quarter Of Leadership* (provided by Ashaway Line and Twine Manufacturing Company, circa 1949)
99 Joseph D. Bates, Jr., *What's New in Fishing Lines* (Field & Stream Magazine, December, 1947)
100 Bruce W. Richards, *Modern Fly Lines*, (Birmingham, Alabama: Odysseus Editions, 1994)
101 Information contained in L. P. Martuch Patent 3,043,045
102 http://www.westegg.com/inflation/
103 Interview with Tom Irvin of 3M
104 Information contained in L. P. Martuch Patent 3,043,045
105 Information contained in J. E. Stark Patent 5,207,732
106 Mark Sosin, *Practical Light-Tackle Fishing* (Garden City, NY: Nick Lyons Books-Doubleday & Co.,1979)
107 Bruce W. Richards, *Modern Fly Lines*, (Birmingham, Alabama: Odysseus Editions, 1994)
108 Patent Number 3,868,785 dated March, 1975
109 Interviews with Danny Foote
110 Interviews with Danny Foote
111 Patent Number 5,207,732 dated May 4, 1993
112 Interviews with Danny Foote
113 James W. Havstad, *Sink Rates of Sinking Lines*, (The Fly Fisher Magazine, 1979)
114 Cortland 444 Sinking Line
115 Scientific Anglers 2002 Catalog
116 Interviews with Art Agnew of Sunset Line and Twin Company
117 Leon L. Martuch, *A History of Scientific Anglers from 1945 to 1973* (Personal manuscript written in February 1996)
118 *Scientific Anglers Golden Anniversary*, (Fishing Tackle Trade News, August 1994)
119 Interview with Tom Irvin of 3M
120 Correspondence with Jean Kohn
121 Interview with Bruce Richards of Scientific Anglers

REFERENCES

122 http://www.suntimes.com/ebert/ebert_reviews/1992/10/782296.html
123 *Fly-fishing allure catches CEO's devotion*, USA Today (June 21, 2002)
124 June 11, 2003 correspondence with Paumanok Publications, Inc.
125 http://www.buildinggreen.com/features/pvc/pvc.html
126 Interview with Bob Goodale of Monic
127 Bruce W. Richards, *Modern Fly Lines*, (Birmingham, Alabama: Odysseus Editions, 1994)
128 Patent Number 5,625,976 dated May 6, 1997
129 Patent Number 5,207,732 dated May 4, 1993
130 Patent Number 6,321,483 dated November 27, 2001
131 Patent Number 6,167,650 dated January 2, 2001
132 Interview with Jim Vincent of Rio
133 Material furnished by Kitty Pearson Vincent
134 Interview with Gareth Jones of Airflo
135 http://www.fg50.com/meet_the_firms/top50.htm#bvg
136 Interview with Bob Goodale of Monic
137 Interview with Rick Tramer of Northern Sport Fishing Products, Ltd.
138 Interview with Jim Teeny of Jim Teeny Inc.
139 http://www.asf.ca/ConservCentre/HallFame/Awardpages/lwulff.html
140 http://www.asf.ca/Communications/Feb99/JWulff.html
141 Interview Doug Cummings of Royal Wulff
142 http://www.orvis.com/detail.asp?subject=9&index=1
143 Leigh Perkins, *A Sportman's Life* (Atlantic Monthly Press)
144 Interview with Jim Lepage of The Orvis Company
145 http://www.llbean.com/customerService/aboutLLBean/timeline.html
146 http://www.cabelas.com/cabelas/en/templates/community/aboutus/history.jhtml?rid=5000151022802
147 Interview with Larry Whiteley of Bass Pro Shops
148 http://www.outdoorworld.com/site/index.cfm

INDEX

A River Runs Through It 128
Abbey & Imbrie 57
Abercrombie & Fitch 56,89,90
Abu 83,84
Acetate 93
Adams Angling 155
Agnew, Art 35,38,103,108,109,117
Airflo 133-135
Allcocks and Youngs 66
American Fishing Tackle Manufacturers
    Assoc. (AFTMA) 7,107,108,109,110,117
American Line Company 57,95
Amnesia Monofilament 38
Angell, Mrs. Billie Boyce 54
Aqualine 73
Aquanova 138,139
Ashaway 8,23,24-27
B. F. Gladding & Company ....
    52-56,121,122,123
Barnes, Dale 82
Bass Pro Shops 152
Bedell, Berkley 78
Beni Hasan 9
Berkley 78-80,82
Bevin Wilcox 47,48
Bombyx Mori 13
Braiding 17
British Insulated Callender Cables
    (BICC) 76,77
Bronson 56
Brooks, Joe 33,103
Burgess, Paul 113
Cabela's 150,151
Carothers, Wallace 93
Castro, Fidel 75,76
Catch and Release 118,119
Chandler, Leon ....
    7,70,71,72,103,108,111,117,153,154
Cilestone Process (Cilesto) 55
Claudius Aelian 9
Clement, George 108
Cleopatra 9
Coating Adhesion 115
Cortland 333 Line 7,71,97
Cortland Line Company ....
    7,68-74,76,77,97,124,130
Cotton 16
Cotton Gin 16
Crandall, Bob 108
Crandall, J. T. 25,26
Crandall's American Finish Line 25,26,156
Cutter, Vic 82
Cuttyhunk 24
Cuttyhunk Fishing Club 24
Dacron 13,33,94
Davis, Wynn 110,103
Distribution of fly lines 119,120
Double Taper lines 12,131
Dougherty, Jack 107,108
Duback, Earl 131,147
E. K. Tyron 119,120
Eaton and Deller 11
Ebay 155
Edgar Sealey and Sons, Ltd. 56

Edwards, Tommy 103,107
Enameled Coatings 17,18
Environmental Concerns 118
Ethylene Acrylic Acid Copolymers ... 131,136
Extrusion Line Coating Process 113
Fenwick 82,83
Fiberglass Fly Rods 5
Flax 16
Flo Tek, Inc. 131,135
Flotation 115
Fly Line Cleaners 157
Fly Line Dressings 19-21,157
Fly Line Dryers 18,157
Foote, Danny R. 79,80,112
Frost, Carrie 43,44
Frothing Technology 116
Gaddis, Gadabout 92
Garcia 84
Gel Spun Polyethylene 130,136
Golden Gate Angling & Casting Club
    (GGACC) 36,37,103,104,105,106
Goodrich, Dr. B. F. 66
Green, Jimmy 36,51,103
Gregory, Myron 36,38,103-110,117
Grey, Zane 24
Gudebrod, Inc. 27-30,77
Halford, Frederick 11
Hall Line Corporation 39-41
Hardisty, Ben 65,68
Hargreaves, James 16
Harris, Clare 121,123
Hedge, Marvin 42,50,51
Hemingway, Ernest 75,76
Henkin, Harmon 5
Hennings, Ivar 59,60
Henshall, Dr. James A. 43,44
Herter, George 90,91
Herter's 90,91
Hewitt, Edward R. 15,19
Horrocks Ibbotson 57-59
Horton Manufacturing Company ....
    71,85,84,86
Hoyle, Pete 71,72
International Braid 41
J. C. Higgins 37,87
Jewett, Lewis 126
Johnson, Red 155
Johnson, Sir William 11
Johnson, Victor Jr. 6,7,166
Johnson, Victor Sr. 6
K. P. Morritt, Ltd. 56
Kauss, Del 126
Kerridge Angling Collection 103
Kevlar 13,111,133
King Eider lines (English) 147,156
Kingfisher lines (English) 11,156
Kingfisher Lines (U.S.) 84,85,86,156
Kmart 119,120
Koller, Larry 10
L.L. Bean 148-150
Lead 118,130
Leisenring, James 21
Len Codella's Sporting Collectibles 155
Lepage, Jim 147

Level Lines 12
Line Memory 114
Line Size Standard 13,102
Line Walk 23
Linen 16,18
Linseed Oil Coatings 18
Malloch, P. D. 11
Marathon 81
Martin Keane's Classic Rods and Tackle,
    Inc. 155
Martin, Jack 76
Martuch, Leon L. 123
Martuch, Leon P. ....
    7,98,100,103,108,112,117,121-123,126
Masterline 28,73,76,77
Maurice Sporting Goods 119
McClane, A. J. 94
Microballoons 99,100,101,115,116,123
Minnesota Mining and Manufacturing
    Company (3M) 65,124,125,126
Monic 131,135,136,137
Monofilament Nylon Braid 111,131
Montgomery Ward 37,70,87
Mucilin 19
Multifilament Nylon Braid 111
New England Butt Company 17
Newton Line Company 73,74-76
Northern Sport Fishing Products, Ltd. ....
    138,139
Norwich Line Company 49-51
Nylon 13,26,93,94,95
Old Hi 95
Oreno 60
Organosol 96
Orvis 77,131,145-147
Outdoors Technologies Group 80,82,84,86
Payne Rod 56,168
Perkins, Leigh 146
Pflueger 66-68
Plasticizer 96,100,112,114,115,153,154
Plastisol 96
Plutarch 9
Polyethylene Copolymers 130
Polyurethane 78,81,113,133
Polyvinyl Chloride (PVC) ....
    65,79,96,97,98,112,130
Price Guide 158-160
PVC Line Coating Process 112
Rain-Beau 41-43
Rayon 93
Richards, Bruce 126,127
Rio 132,133
Ritz, Charles 103
Rope Walk 52
Rottiers, Paul 121
Royal Wulff 142-144
Ryobi Limited 77
S. A. Jones Line Company 49
Saunder, John 15
Schindler Company 41
Schultz, Arne 103,107
Schuykill Fishing Club 23
Schwiebert, Ernest 9

INDEX

Scientific Anglers (SA) ....
.... 5,7,27,55,56,71,121-127
Sealand 41
Sears Roebuck and Company 87,88
Semon, Waldo 96
Shakespeare 63-66
Shakespeare, William Jr. 63
Shapleigh and Simmons 119
Shootability 114
Shooting Head Lines 12,37
Silk 13,14
Silk Gut 15
Sinking Lines 116,117,118
Skues, G.E.M. 21
Smith, Ray 68
Soo Valley Line Company 59,63,65,99
Sosin, Mark 103,110
South Bend 56,59-62,70
Spinning Jenny 16
Stark, John 126
Sunset 35-38,77
Supthin, Harry 108
Tarintino, Jon 36,103
Teeny Nymph Company 140-142
Teeny, Jim A. 140-142
Teflon 113,131,133,134,138
The Compleat Angler 10
Torpedo Taper lines 12,13
Trilene 78
Trout Unlimited 119
Trueblood, Ted 103,107,108
Tungsten 118,134
U.S. Line Company 30-33
U.S. Whip Company 30
Wal-Mart 119,120
Walton, Izaak 10
Ward, Richard 108
Wattford, Thomas 17
Weber Lifelike Fly Company 43,45
Weber, Oscar 43,44
Weight Forward Lines 12,131
Western Auto Supply 37,70,87,88
Western Fishing Line Company 33-35
Whitlock, Dave 5
Whitney, Eli 16
Williams, Ted 65,88
Wolff, Dick 84
Wulff, Joan 142,144
Wulff, Lee 18,84,103,142,144

ABOUT THE AUTHOR

Victor Johnson, Jr. is a Civil Engineer who lives in Vallejo, California. The photo is Victor and his wife, Sarah, on a fishing trip to Mexico in 2002. The Johnson's also have two daughters, Elizabeth and Kristine.